Wood Songs

A Folksinger's
Social Commentary, Cook Manual

Song Book

by
Michael Johnathon

𝔚ood𝔖ongs
A Folksinger's Social Commentary
Cook Manual 🍁 Song Book

published by
NORTH AMERICAN IMPRINTS
Oscar Rucker, publisher
P.O. Box 337, Berea, KY 40403

Music Transcriptions by
John Roberts
1605 Lenox Road, Schenectady, NY 12308

"Sunlight In Trees" *front and back cover photo by* **Warren Brunner**
"Maple Leaf Woodcut" *by* **Homer Ledford,** *Photo by* **Harold Roth**

ISBN#
0-935680-66-7

Library of Congress Catalog Card #
96-070333

A book by Michael Johnathon
WoodSongs: A Folksinger's Social Commentary, Cook Manual and Song Book
An original collection of commentaries, short stories, poetry,
songs with music and tableture, and recipes.

**"I'm more amazed at the varied meanings of words
and more suspicious of adjectives than ever..."**
Carl Sandburg, poet and writer

Wood Songs

An Introduction

It's music that comes from the wood...

It's a spirit and a feeling.
It's a sense of nature.
It's a log cabin and a garden.
It's a fresh summer salad with tomatoes and cucumbers picked just this morning.
It's a walk in the woods along a forest brook in October while holding hands with your lifemate.
It's a poem easily remembered that rolls off your tongue at the right moment to the right person.
It's flannel pajamas on a snowy New England night with the fireplace cracklin' all warm and cozy while reading a good book.
It's a guitar and a poem and a song and a canvas and a sculpture and a dream and a vision all wrapped up together like a fresh baked batch of homemade cookies, ready to share.

When I recorded the *WoodSongs* album, I wanted it to be all of these things in a musical sense.

Now comes the *WoodSongs* book.

The challenge was to take all these feelings that I so easily interpret musically and try to transpose them into words. It was a difficult venture. I mean, I know how to *sing* these things to people, but could I *write* them on paper?

I had a decision to make:

To write a novel, a made-up story in a world saturated with myriads of made-up stories . . .

Or, to write a book that could give you a little piece of the world I am from without being another boring autobiography.

So, *WoodSongs: A Folksinger's Social Commentary, Cook Manual & Song Book* was born. This book is not about me, really. Sure, I use my point of view a good deal. After all, it's the only one I've got. Still, this is clearly not an autobiography. It's a book of thought, and of song, of poetry and of good food.

WoodSongs is about everybody.

Even you.

And your children.

It's about writing your own songs and trying old things new again. It's about seeing without using your eyes and hearing without using your ears. It's about touching and thinking and changing your mind. It's a fun place to be.

Musically, *WoodSongs* is about finding the soul of a song by searching out the heart of the wood. As a book, it's about seeking the pulse of the future by searching out the spirit of the past.

WoodSongs approaches tomorrow by taking a step backward in time. It's sort of a *USA Today* meets *Mother Earth News*, with music of course. And some really good recipes.

WoodSongs looks at the world strictly from a folksinger's point of view. It's a book of my own design, my own inspiration and for my own purpose.

I also wrote it for other songwriters and artists who struggle through each day trying to find another reason to press on. I applaud them all. It's for working men and women trying to find purpose within their families, who come home each day to bills and frustrations, with the TV blaring in the background each evening like some crazy soundtrack to their life.

It's something I wrote to give to my daughter, Melody. She is a precious part of my life who is facing the hardest part of hers. I do not envy any child beginning their teenage journey during the closing years of this century. Or for any kids who spend each afternoon isolated up in their rooms at home, listening to the same record over and over again, lost in their confusion. It's OK, we all did that.

WoodSongs is for anybody who likes the idea of tradition being part of their future. It's for those who like chopping wood in the winter time. It's for apartment dwellers who dream of their own cabin or farm. It's for those who like to sing while planting a spring time garden. It's for those who choose NPR over MTV, who place people over money, family over careers, dreams over reality, hemp over tobacco, home cooked meals over fast food, reusing over recycling, a fireplace over a VCR, homemade music over Top 40 radio, and who listen closely to the dreams of their children.

And it's for those who enjoy a good laugh, a good glass of red wine late at night, and a hot cup of coffee in the morning. It's for those who linger at their lover's bedside at sunrise to watch them wake up.

I guess my point is this,

WoodSongs is written in the hope of making you a little happier by not taking our self-inflicted worldly pains so seriously. I want it to be an entertaining way to get you to sing, and draw, and create. I don't care if it's music, art or cooking...so long as you're having fun.

This world of ours is squeezed up tighter than a gnat's ass on an ice cube... it's too tense around here! I think it's time we get back to reality, to relax and enjoy life a little. Life is too short to be worrying about half the stuff we fret over nowadays.

So, play an old record on your hi-tech Victrola, go buy a banjo, plant a garden or sing a good song...maybe one of your own.

Or, better yet, do it all!

Folk On!

Dedicated to Melody Larkin

"My life is lived with ease...
I know not the first letter of the alphabet"
Henry David Thoreau

"This job is a challenge...you have to know
all the letters of the alphabet..."
Vanna White

"You forgot the 'e' at the end of
the word Potato..."
Vice President Dan Quayle

Appalachia

There is a quiet sense of family in Appalachia.

It permeates the mountains like the sound of a coal train rolling gently between two hollows. It's like the smell of an early summer lilac bush that entangles you while sitting on your front porch during an afternoon rain.

Strong.

Ever present.

You know when it's there. You miss it when it's gone. It leaves no question that it shall return.

I'm writing this part of the *WoodSongs* book while sitting on the porch of folksinger Jean Ritchie's log cabin in Viper, Kentucky. If you can picture this, I'm sitting on an old, wooden rocking chair with a pen and writing tablet in hand. In front of me, the side of this huge mountain is framed by the cabin's back porch. I'm actually listening to a train rumble along in a far off holler. I can smell the fragrance of the lilac bush that Jean's mother planted years ago, just 50 feet away from me.

And a gentle rain falls.

Jean and I have spent a good part of this Sunday together, on our way to a show in Whitesburg, Kentucky. I enjoy spending time with Jean. She is such a sweet lady who has, along with her husband George and two sons John and Peter, traveled the world singing the ballads of Appalachia. She has a beautiful voice and she's a magnificent songwriter.

And she loves her family.

For most of our trip today, as we drove through the mountains and small Appalachian towns, Jean told me stories about her family and relatives from times past. It's as if each one, though perhaps dead and gone long ago, still lives with a bright smile deep within her memory. And she shares those memories so freely and gently.

We stopped to rest up here at her family cabin outside of Hazard. It's a grand place, made of very old hand hewn logs. Built strong and forever and with a purpose. Inside, it brims with Jean and George's life. Old quilts line the couches and chairs, soft feather mattresses on the beds and pictures of family members from generations ago. Musical instruments and songbooks are piled high on an old foot pedal organ in the corner of a great living room. George's handmade spiral staircase that leads up to a loft and some of his photographs act as centerpieces for the house.

Jean and I spent some time on this porch for a while today, sipping a cold drink as she talked on about the old stories of her family, her sister Edna and her travels around the globe. As I listened, it made me wonder what stories I could tell you, my unknown reader. What words and experiences could I relay in this book, this great opportunity given me, that could compare with the sweetness and life of Jean Ritchie?

So, I sit on this porch writing these very thoughts down. Jean has gone inside for a while, but I stay here, parked on her old wooden rocking chair listening to the rain fall on the trees and on the cabin roof. I listen to that train fade away in the distance and it reminds me of the years when I once lived in these very mountains not too far from here, and of the music I heard and the people I've since come to miss.

It's that feeling of "missing" that is grabbing me right now. The mountains are so beautiful today. They look so musical. But they ache at me, just the same. The mountains remind me of what I miss. For me, they are a family of mine, telling me stories as I gaze at them, not unlike the stories Jean tells of her family.

It was this very idea of family that sent me on my own journey into these mountains to become a folksinger, not so very long ago.

As a kid, I grew up around acoustic music, especially while attending school in upstate New York. Like most other teenagers, my days pretty much revolved around the records spinning on the stereo in my room, or playing the guitar till late at night while the rest of my family watched TV. I did the rock band thing in school for a while and wrote tons of poetry. Drawing, music, plays and painting...I loved it all and did it all. I even had my own cartoon strip published in a regional newspaper in Poughkeepsie, New York. Not bad for a sixteen year old kid.

By the early 1980's, I moved from my New York home and got a job as a disc jockey in Laredo, Texas (which I'll tell you more about later in this book). Late one night, while at the radio station, I was playing an old record by The Byrds called *Turn, Turn, Turn*.

As the song played on the turntable, I noticed on the record sleeve that the tune was written by Pete Seeger and God. I've since come to appreciate that it was only appropriate that Pete Seeger would be God's co-writer.

Anyway, as the song played, I recalled seeing Pete Seeger perform an environmental concert along the shores of the Hudson River near the town of Fishkill, where I lived. Our high school science class went to the concert as sort of a field trip to visit the sloop Clearwater. Pete and some of his friends built the old-style wooden colonial ship to bring attention to the pollution along the river. The idea was to use the Clearwater and music concerts to get folks to come to the river. Once they saw what had happened to their river, Pete and the Clearwater folks believed they would do what was needed to clean it up on their own.

About two thousand rabid teenagers assembled that day on the river banks waiting for this concert to start. We were a bunch of hormone enraged teenagers into rock bands like The Eagles and Kiss. Then this skinny dude with a...a...*banjo* gets up on stage.

Well, we were ready to chew ol' Pete Whats-his-face up and spit him out into the river for fish food. Then he starts playing this song about how school sucks, or something. Anyway, in two minutes flat he had a couple thousand teenagers singing good and loud.

I was completely amazed and blown away by the experience. I had never seen so much power cradled in such a simple manner.

Pete won us over with just his voice and his song. We could tell Pete actually cared about us and about this old river. By the time we left that day, he had us humming "school sucks" while we picked up garbage along the Hudson shoreline. The feeling of that day was branded in my memory and stayed with me for years afterward.

This particular night at the radio station, the image of Pete singing on that little riverfront stage (and of Mary Ann DeArce as she bent over in her tight jeans picking up Pepsi cans), filtered through my mind as the song ended.

> *To everything Turn, Turn, Turn*
> *There is a season Turn, Turn, Turn...*

By the time the record was over, I decided that my "season" for searching had come. I wanted to find the simple, raw power that Pete used to touch us that day on the Hudson River shoreline. It was time for me to find myself, my past and my future by searching for my music.

I had reasons to feel this way.

Because, basically, I am a man with no past.

My father died five days before I was born.

My mother, who remarried eleven months later, was a very hurt and troubled woman. I grew up in an alcoholic household, ripped apart by very violent fighting. The fighting and alcoholism caused me to draw inward.

My stepfather had a hard time dealing with me because I

11

wasn't his son, and my mother used me to vent her anger and pain over her life's situation. My relatives were polarized, either on mom's side or my stepfather's, and most of their attention was focused on my younger brother and sister, as they were at least the products of both parents. I was an older, angry black sheep stuck in the middle of an angry war between two parents with a dump truck load of troubles.

She wasn't happy.

He wasn't happy.

And I was a kid who just wished *somebody* would explain to me who my real father was.

I spent most of my youth like a lot of troubled kids. Upstairs in my room, alone. I would draw, play lots of records, and write stories. I also learned how to play the guitar. At one point, my artwork became so good that a regional newspaper bought 12 weekly cartoon strips from me.

Hey, I was only 16 years old and some newspaper sent me a check for $150 in advance. Cool! I remember being out of my mind with excitement after reading their letter to me. I ran downstairs clutching the letter in one hand and the check in the other to show my mom and stepfather. My mom's reaction was to go into my room, tear down all my artwork off the walls and burn it in the backyard.

So much for family encouragement, I figured.

It became obvious to me quickly that anything I did would have to be on my own. So, I settled further into my own head. Most of my solace was found in music. I would stay up late into the night with the headphones on, listening to the same albums a hundred times. Artists like Josh White, David Gates, Dan Fogelberg, Neil Young, Big Bill Broonzy and others became my daily companions.

Lack of affection and no sense of "family" was compounded by the fact that I grew up using the wrong name, and didn't even know it until I was in junior high school. I didn't realize I wasn't my "father's" son until I was about thirteen years old. I was inadvertently informed during the middle of a huge, loud and violent argument between my parents.

What? This man I grew up with is not my father?

And nobody was going to explain this?

Ever?

I swear, you could have sliced me in half with a dull ax and it would have hurt less. So, why was I using my stepfather's name, I wondered? For most of my teenage years, I often questioned why he never adopted me. I later discovered that doing so would have stopped about $600 a month in support payments from my real dad's estate. Not that we were hurting; my stepfather was a very successful and respected executive for a big national company. Looking back, it probably was the smart thing to do...I just wish it had been explained to me.

I think mostly it was a pride thing. My stepfather seemed to be very uncomfortable with the idea that I wasn't his. And the intense

12

friction he had with my mother didn't help the matter. He had me use his name to save face, which was OK except all my legal papers were still in my real dad's name. It made life extremely awkward, like during graduation when the principal called out a strange name that no one had ever heard of before and I came walking up to collect the diploma.

I also couldn't understand why not a single one of my real dad's relatives, none of his sisters, brothers or cousins, ever tried to contact me.

Me, his only child.

Or so I was told.

This is not a good thing for a teenager to go through, you know what I mean? Not while you're trying to find your way in the world.

But that's how I entered adult life. Pissed off, confused and not belonging anywhere...stuck with using a name I didn't even know I had until recently.

The first thing I did as an adult, I mean *immediately* after graduating from high school, was totally drop my stepfather's name. It wasn't that I was ashamed or hated anybody. To the contrary, I appreciated all my parents had done for me. I was certainly provided for during my whole youth. But I wanted to start finding *me*... something I always wondered about. I didn't have much to fall back on, as I didn't know any of my own history and nobody would ever tell me anything.

So I just dropped it all.

I simply canceled the past out of my mind and started to create a legacy that would begin with *me*.

The second thing I did was decide I was not going to college. I didn't feel a university could teach me the things I wanted to know. I never did really think too highly of school, even though I was a consistent "A" student. In my humble opinion, colleges are nothing more than huge bars with a $28,000 cover charge. Life, it seemed to me, was a much better teacher. And cheaper.

Josh White

Stringbean

Woody Guthrie

The third thing I did, also right out of high school, was marry a wonderful woman even more confused than I was. Her first husband, a friend of mine, killed himself by drinking poison just ten months earlier, and so here I was walking down the aisle with the widow. I guess I wanted to share my new name with someone really quick. Even though we have long since parted, she and I remain good friends to this day, jointly raising our daughter, Melody.

But, at the time, I could only see two things. The first was being with someone who needed me.

It felt sort of like love. Close enough for me, anyway.

The other was I wanted to get away from home.

Fast.

As far away from the fighting and the stress as I could get. I took my new bride, still draped in a maze of her own confusion, put her in a car, and drove 44 hours straight until I got to Laredo, Texas where some friends helped me get a gig as a radio disc jockey.

And so, as fate would have it, here I was in Laredo several months later...on the air late at night listening to the final phrases of *Turn, Turn, Turn...* with images of both Pete and my past colliding in my brain.

So, I came up with an idea.

Actually, the idea hit me harder than a sledgehammer.

It was time for me to become a folksinger.

Yes, as glam rock bands like KISS reached their zenith, disco was King and Bon Jovi loomed in the near future, I decided right then and there that *folk* was gonna be my thing.

No kidding....that's exactly how it happened.

It must have been on my mind for a while. It had to have been. The decision to leave Laredo was not present in my head when the song started, but it was locked in granite by the time it ended.

Don't get me wrong, it wasn't like I was a folk novice or anything. I had a tremendous appetite for the music, and I listened to it all. The Carter Family, Josh White, Woody and Arlo, Harry Chapin, Don McLean, Janis Ian, Odetta and more. I was playing guitar and banjo and writing songs all the time. My musical skills were increasing and I was playing in public more and more. I loved this artform with a passion and read about it constantly. While in high school I would play with bands or just by myself, recorded my songs in studios and even performed live several times on radio shows. I thought it was just a hobby, but I guess it meant a lot more to me.

I really wanted to write and sing about things that were important to me. All the seeds were there, just waiting to be watered.

Turn, Turn, Turn hit me like a summer thundercloud.

You see, with folk music, I was able to touch a part of life that didn't belong to me.

Tradition.

A past.

It was that very sense of belonging to a long line of *anything*

14

that had a very calming effect on me. Woody and Stringbean and Uncle Dave Macon could become my musical family. The stories of their songs and lives could become the stories of my history.

Hey, I had none of my own, so why not?

Three months later, all my stuff was packed and I was on the road to Mousie, Kentucky to be a folksinger.

Why Mousie, of all places, you ask?

Well, let me tell you about that.

By the time I got home from the radio station that night in Laredo, I had things pretty much thought out. I tend to work that way, you know. I make decisions fast and then shoot from the hip. I can get a lot done quickly that way. I learned from my youth the value of self motivation, so I was ready to start. And I also knew that Appalachia was the grand breeding ground for the music I loved most, so that's where I had to go.

Right *now*.

A few weeks later, I made a quick trip to Whitesburg, Kentucky in Letcher county to visit some friends I knew and to check the area out for a few days. In Whitesburg, there is a great place called Appalshop, sort of an Appalachian version of the Smithsonian Institute. They've collected songs and stories from mountain folks for decades, preserving them on film and on records. You can take your family there for literally the entire day and still not want to leave. I encourage everyone reading this to take a trip to the mountains and make Appalshop part of the visit, especially if you're from Appalachia. Do this as part of your family heritage. You owe this to yourself and to your kids...and you *won't* be disappointed!

One guy, who still works there, a brilliant filmmaker named Herbie Smith, produced 16mm films about mountain life. One film, called *Hand Carved, is* about a mountain man who walks into the woods with an ax and a saw and comes out with a finished rocking chair. It's a great film...kind of like watching an issue of *Mother Earth News* magazine come to life. What's really amazing is that you can go to Appalshop to watch this great film while sitting in the very chair you're watching being made!

My friends in Whitesburg and I decided we wanted to go out to dinner and discuss this big move of mine into the Appalachian mountains. We hopped in the car and traveled out of Letcher County into Knott County on old Hiway 80, heading to a restaurant in Pike County *(there were not many restaurants in the mountains, if you can't tell)*.

So, we're cruising down the road and we go past a sign on the road that says "Mousie". Well, yours truly HAS to stop and check out what the heck a "Mousie" is.

Mousie was a bend in the road.

Period.

And I loved it!

It was a small hamlet of folks who lived across the mountain from Hindman, the county seat. Mousie was made up of the Mousie

Market, the Mousie post office, Wicker's Gulf station and Ansel Campbell's General Store.

Now, Ansel Campbell was a sight indeed.

I walked into his general store, which was an old fieldstone building filled high with shelves stocked with plow parts, nails, hardware, soaps and even a box of ladies girdles with a 1946 postmark still on the box. It was a grand, old-timey looking building with oiled wood floors and an old heat stove in the center. Ansel sat next to the stove in a wicker chair, dressed in work boots, coveralls and an old flannel shirt. He had on his Red Rooster baseball cap and was spitting tobacco into a Maxwell House coffee can at his feet.

"Howdy, neighbor," he said as I walked in.

I felt like I had just entered a Norman Rockwell painting of early America come to life, sort of a folk *Twilight Zone.*

I was home, and I knew it.

And Ansel became my landlord that afternoon. He had a piece of property just outside of Mousie, on the other side of the bend in the road, for rent. It was a little place built on a cut-out, perched on the side of a mountain. It was on 26 acres of land, a house with a work shop and some bottom land for a garden, a fresh water well and situated right off a paved road.

For $125 bucks a month.

A few weeks later, I moved in.

What I moved into was a world unlike anything I had ever seen before. The culture of Appalachia was a complete inversion of what I had experienced in south Texas, and Laredo was completely upside down from what I grew up with in New York. I may have been a fish out of water, but I was growing legs fast.

Actually, I was too stupid to know I didn't belong there. And the people were too sweet and nice to tell me. So, I settled in, fixed up my house and set about to the task of learning how to be a folksinger.

Photos courtesy of Appalshop

Scenes from Herbie Smith's film, "Hand Carved"

First thing I did was start soaking up the music of the area. I met people like Ray Sloane, who with his family ran a small music store. Ray was a banjo picker, a good one, and he introduced me to the music of The McLain Family Band, Sparky Rucker, I.D. Stamper and others. Ray also introduced me to Doug Hutcheons who worked at Alice Lloyd College in Pippa Passes, not far from Mousie. Doug is a great banjo player and instrument maker, was formerly one of Bill Monroe's Bluegrass Boys and is currently a field rep for the Gibson Guitar Company.

I learned a lot of banjo licks and songs from Doug. I was sitting in his apartment one day reading a three year old issue of FRETS Magazine *(this was over a year after they ceased publication)* and found a banjo for sale in the classified section. It was an original Vega long neck, the PS5 classic...Wow! I wondered out loud if a banjo like that was available in Kentucky somewhere. Doug, who was also a world class instrument trader said "not likely...you should call the number in the ad."

Call a three year old classified ad?

Shucks, why not...

So I did.

The guy answered the phone, stammered a bit; he couldn't believe I was calling three years after he placed that ad but, yes, he still had the banjo locked up in the case in his closet.

Three days later, my banjo arrived in a UPS truck.

So, here I was, Michael Johnathon the folk singer from Mousie, Kentucky with my Martin D35s guitar and Vega PS5 long neck banjo. I had a little house with a garden, a bunch of songs and a lot of energy. I had everything a folksinger could possibly need...

...except gigs.

But I didn't care.

I was foot loose and fiance' free.

So, each morning I would grab my guitar and banjo, toss them in the back of my small pickup truck and roam down a holler. I would knock on a door, tell the folks I was trying to learn some old songs and could they teach me one? Well, word gets out real fast in the hills, and news about this crazy New York kid with his guitar had been passed around pretty quickly. It was not uncommon to be invited into someone's house or sit on their porch as they pulled out a fiddle or an old guitar, maybe old scratchy records, and we would play and sing these great old songs. I learned dozens of versions of *Redwing* and *Cripple Creek.*

Music, I have found, takes on tremendous meaning to people when money is *not* involved. None of the folks I sang with when I was in Mousie cared a thing about being a star, or looking good, or image, or even if they were perfectly in tune. The songs were part of their family. The music settled against their skin like a good pair of worn underwear.

Clean ones, of course.

I never did hear any dirty songs in Appalachia.

Another friend of mine, Mike Mullins, ran the Hindman Settlement School. They would host small music programs, called "house concerts" and invite singers like Lee Sexton, Si Kahn and others to perform. One night, they had a concert by a dulcimer player and songwriter named John McCutcheon. During the show, he played a song called *Gone, Gonna Rise Again,* otherwise known as *New Wood.* That song, written by Si Kahn, seemed to capture the reason why I moved to Appalachia in its lyrics and I've kept that song as part of my show ever since. It was a grand thrill for me, years later, to finally record *New Wood* as part of the CD *Assassins In The Kingdom* with my friend Odetta singing the duet with me.

Not too infrequently, my "New Yorkness" would show. Sort of like a pimple poking through on prom night. It only came around when I was guaranteed to look as bad as possible.

It was my habit to spend a warm evening on a hillside by my house overlooking a long holler. Across the holler, I could see clearly old John Wicker's little farmstead, maybe four acres of corn fields and an old barn. The bottom was completely surrounded by the mountains, so you always had this feeling that you were living in a big hallway without any ceilings.

Anyway, I'm sitting on a log reading a book and I look up to see old John plowing his field with his mule Bill. Mr. Wicker was a tough, spry 75 year old fellow with a thin, hard shelled little body. A lot like his mule. As a matter of fact, the only real difference I saw between John and Bill was that Bill never spit tobacco on my shoes while visiting with me.

I watched John plowing his field and came to a forthright decision that, yes, I Michael Johnathon would also set about to plow my garden with a mule, too.

"Well, well, well..." old John must have thought as I asked him if I could borrow his mule, *"...this ought to be a good show."*

The next day, John brought Bill across the road to my place, put me behind the plow, handed me the reigns and said, *"Don't forget to let Bill help you some."*

For the next two hours, I felt like I was riding a bull through an earthquake as old John sat on a pail, whittled on a stick of wood and watched Mr. New York Hotshot plow my little half-acre garden with his mule.

Needless to say, I went to bed early that night.

And the folks in town didn't see much of me for several days afterward as I tried to relearn basic human functions...like walking, raising my hand above my head, blinking my eyelids without screaming in pain...

...things like that.

However, it is with great pride that I can write, years later, that I did in fact plow that garden with a mule. And I did it by myself. I planted corn and beans and tomatoes and watermelons in that garden and passed them around to my neighbors with pride.

Of course, at the time I thought the smile on their faces was in gratitude for the fresh vegetables I gave them as gifts. It never occurred to me that the story of me, John, and his mule Bill, had made the rounds throughout the county, and in several enhanced versions thereof, by the time I delivered my garden bounty.

It's things like that, though, that help earn your acceptance into a new community. My mountain neighbors knew I was harmless, even though I was from the north. They generously forgave me for that, for which I am grateful. I simply let it be known that, even though I was *transplanted*, I was *homegrown*. The local folks watched me learning their songs, learning their gardening and lifestyles...and concluded that I was respectable enough.

Most mornings, it was my routine to head into Hindman and have breakfast at a small cafe' on Main Street. Outside the cafe', a small field stone building that was a combination drug store and restaurant, was an eight foot long railroad tie where the old men would gather each morning. About five or six fellas would sit, spit and whittle while sharing their wisdom regarding the news of the day, local politics and county gossip. They were a hoot to listen to. They would carry on about *"thet ol' dye haired actor fella who's presy-dent"* or taxes. They would issue wisdom on the youth of America and the best time of day to milk a cow (*"...whenever she's good 'n ready"* was the conclusion) all in the same sentence.

Each morning, I would have breakfast, read the paper and have coffee. As I would leave the café, I would stop and briefly say hello to the old gentlemen on the bench, maybe chat a few minutes, and then move on to the rest of my day.

One morning, about a week or two after I had plowed my garden with Bill, I greeted the old men as I usually did when I walked out onto the sidewalk.

I said, "Hi."

The old men stopped talking and looked up at me.

They paused a minute.

Then, all at once, the five of 'em moved down one space on the

Typical east Kentucky general store

bench to make a place for me. It was at that very instant, as the men slid down a spot, that I knew I had finally and officially become *local*.

Local!

I just loved the idea of it. I felt like Arlo Guthrie sitting on the Group W bench in his *Alice's Restaurant* song (of course, unlike Arlo, I still had my pants on).

I remember, as I sat on that railroad tie in the middle of Hindman, Kentucky, how unusual this feeling of "belonging" was to me. It was warm and poetic...and it scared me a little. It made me want more of something I wasn't used to having. I knew I wanted to keep it, but I didn't know how. We sat there that morning and let time pass by like the cars in the road. I was living in a moment of the old men's lives, something they did each and every day, but to me it was brand new.

I was comfortably uncomfortable.

Like I feel right now as I sit on Jean Ritchie's cabin porch and write these pages. I'm sitting in a beautiful spot that has been enjoyed by others for years and years. I am new here and living in a moment of someone else's tradition, making it my own, even if only for a few minutes.

I mean, it's the same mountain that was viewed by someone else a generation ago. The mountain has barely changed, but the times have. The sound of the rain is the same on the cabin roof as it was decades ago. But the rain is *new* rain, isn't it?

That's what I'm feeling at this moment. It's a brand new feeling regarding something very old.

The oldest and greatest tradition of Appalachia is it's passionate love for family. Your "people" as it's called. Jean continues to reflect that tradition in her songs and stories as she travels around the world. She keeps the old ways alive in her music, even as we face a brand new century. And no matter what she is doing, her thoughts and her conversation are never too far away from the idea of family. Every song she sings and each story she tells is just a comment away from her momma or her dad. Each song is somehow connected to what she learned from a cousin or an aunt or a friend from the old days when she was growing up in the hills of Perry County. Every award she is given, each event that happens in her life is gently laced with a comment about her husband George, or her sons, John and Peter.

Or her sister Edna. Now *there's* a little sweetie...

It's such a pleasant rain on this Sunday afternoon. I don't want to leave it, but we have to head out for the Whitesburg concert soon. The open arms of the mountains and the soft creak of this rocking chair remind me that, once upon what now seems to be a lifetime ago, for a brief instant in time, I was local.

I belonged here.

I thought it would last forever, too.

Photo by George Pickow

Jean Ritchie

21

Troubadour

Words and Music by
Michael Johnathon
©1991 TechnoFolk Music Group/BMI
as performed on the CD "Troubadour"

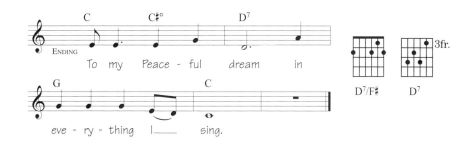

To my   Peace - ful   dream   in

eve - ry - thing   I___   sing.

Troubadour

I hear the song of a Troubadour
My old guitar is hangin' on the wall
The poets live in its wooden soul
In all the songs of long ago.
Golden strings glisten in the sun
Calling everyone to share its glory
Peaceful song, where did you go?
Peaceful song, where did you go?

I save the pictures of the friends that I've known
All my companions of the world
They share my wine and my firelight
I share their smiles and their songs
Through the years I've watched them come and go
Like the winter snow melts the springtime
Peaceful friend, where did you go?
Peaceful friend, where did you go?

And the years go by one by one
And the time slips by you when you're young
And that golden song that you
Hoped for all along to sing
Putting everything into your dream
Peaceful dream in everything I sing

The world trembles at the times that I've known
Through all the war and all the pain
They promise peace and security
But their words just drip like poison rain
Swirling through this computer age,
this Techno-drunken rage without a savior
Peaceful world, where did you go?
Peaceful world, where did you go?

To my peaceful dream
In everything I sing

WoodSongs Cookies

a recipe

When the idea of an acoustic/traditional recording project came around, I had to come up with a name, a phrase that would describe the sound and style of my music. Spending time with my friend Homer Ledford, a master wood craftsman, was all the inspiration I needed. The term *WoodSongs* was born while watching him repair my Martin guitar in his basement workshop. Later that night, I wrote the name *WoodSong* on a piece of paper... and the rest of the album was born.

WoodSongs is a music style, a song, a CD, a newsletter, and now a book...so it might as well be a cookie, too!

The *WoodSongs* cookie is a tasty, natural, whole house treat. And real easy to bake:

1 1/2 cups whole wheat pastry flour	1 1/4 cups rolled oats
1 1/2 cups raisins	1 cup walnuts, chopped
2 eggs	1 cup almonds, chopped
1 cup of honey	1 cup pecans, chopped
1/4 teaspoon ginger	1/2 cup sesame seeds
1/2 teaspoon salt	1/2 cup sunflower seeds, hulled
1 tablespoon baking powder	1 tablespoon cinnamon

1/2 pound real butter, softened (salted or unsalted)
1/2 cup natural peanut butter (don't you *dare* use Skippy)

OK...get yourself a nice big bowl and a sifter. Sift together the baking powder, flour, cinnamon, ginger and salt. Then, toss in the raisins, oats, nuts and seeds.

Next, in a somewhat smaller bowl, mix together the butter, peanut butter, eggs and honey until all the contents are creamy. Then combine the two mixes.

On a flat baking tin, drop about a 1/4 cup for a big cookie, or a wooden spoonful of dough for each medium sized cookie. Make sure you grease the pan well with Crisco. Otherwise, you'll end up with *WoodSongs Crumbs* when you try to get them off!

Bake the cookies at 350 degrees for 18-20 minutes, or until they are golden brown. The cookie itself should be semi-firm, not hard.

Served best in October after chopping firewood while wearing jeans and an old flannel shirt. You and your sweetheart should sit together in front of a warm fireplace with these cookies and some fresh apple cider. If you *really* want something good, try them with a glass of Merlot wine!

Mmmmmm!

Pete

I'm not going to ramble on with a bunch of emotional drivel about why Pete Seeger is the greatest human being on planet earth.

He's not.

Hey, *nobody* is.

But for the past half century, the American public has had a love-hate affair with this guy. He has roamed the planet with his banjo, uncovering songs and passing them on. He was responsible for bringing some of our most important songs to the American consciousness. He marched for civil rights, sailed on behalf of the environment and was banned from American television for nearly two decades because of his political views. He pioneered what performers now call the college circuit, because he couldn't find work, even after selling millions of records.

Music, however, was not a first career choice for Pete.

After college, he tried his hand at journalism, and failed. He attempted to be an artist and painter, and failed. In 1939 he got a job at the World's Fair in New York City as a sort of janitor, a litter picker. His future wife, Toshi Ohta, was a waitress at one of the food pavilions. They've been married now for over half a century.

After two months of "litter picking" Pete saved a few dollars and took off for a summer giving puppet shows through upstate New York. Then he took up the banjo and tried his luck as a musician. When he began his career as a folksinger, it was rough at best. But Pete persevered and made a lot of contacts.

In March of 1940, folk collector Alan Lomax introduced Pete Seeger to another singer, Woody Guthrie. Originally a sign painter from a small town in Oklahoma, Woody was in New York City because actor Will Geer had urged him to come east. Woody's poor Okie background was worlds apart from Pete's, but he took an immediate liking to this tall, skinny banjo player with a proletariat attitude and a big Adam's apple. Both shared a strong passion for music and a thirst for real human experience. So, Pete and Woody (who was seven years older than Pete) decided they would see America by their bootstraps, hitchhiking across the country, often singing together at labor camps and union halls.

Toshi Seeger

Yes, by the way, it's true.

They were communists.

This, of course, was *before* communism was the same as being Russian. Back in the 1940's, communism was an American political party, with candidates running for president and everything. They believed there should be no rich or poor classes of people. Everybody should be equal, have an equal say and get a fair wage for their labors.

At the time, most people in music and the arts in general felt that way. They felt a certain kinship (I think it might have been out of guilt) with the story of the Apostles from the book of Acts who sold all their material possessions and gave all the proceeds to the poor. Artists tend to be a privileged lot. They live by their own rules, get paid well for a limited amount of physical labor and secure a bit of fame in the process.

In 1940, there was plenty for an artist or any other caring person to feel guilty about. And Pete and Woody saw it all first hand as they made their way across America.

Think of what they saw:

The world was on the eve of war for the second time in less than one generation. Nations around the globe chose to pick up arms and fight out their differences instead of negotiating. Reason was thrown to the wind as normally sane men clawed and attacked each other in bloody battles for hazy, unknown reasons. Evil men like Hitler and Mussolini cast their dark shadows upon the masses as millions of innocent people, mostly Jews, were sacrificed at their political whims. On the other end of the globe, Japan would soon flex both its muscles and stupidity by dropping bombs on American soil, sending thousands more young men to their deaths in the Pacific rim.

It would culminate in one of the most violent, frightening and massive explosions in human history.

Here at home, thousands of families were ripped apart as young men lost their lives at war while fighting overseas in strange lands. Huge droughts in the 1930's created the Dust Bowl in the midwest, displacing untold thousands more families from their homes. Across the nation, indeed the world, a crushing economic depression forced millions into soup lines and onto the streets.

Pete and Woody traveled across the country singing to common folks during this time. They saw first hand the hurt and the pain and the confusion in the eyes of the people they met.

Later, as Woody hitchhiked his way back east from their trip, he began writing a song that, unknown to him at the time, would someday affect the lives of millions of people.

He arrived home in New York City, kicked back in his upstairs apartment and allowed the images of the long trip to settle into his mind. At the same time, whenever he turned on the radio a certain hit song sweeping the American airwaves came blasting through, making him uncomfortable each time he heard it.

Irving Berlin had a tune on the Hit Parade called *"God Bless America."* The words of the song cut through Woody like a hot knife.

"God Bless America? What on earth is God blessing?" he wondered.

Woody didn't see *anything* that looked like a blessing to him. Not when millions of Americans were facing the struggle of their lives. After what he had just witnessed on his trip, he was moved to reply to Irving Berlin's song *"God Bless America"* with this new, half-finished song of his own. Woody sat down and did what any good folksinger would do under the circumstances: he pulled out his guitar and completed his protest song, now directing it against Irving Berlin's tune. He wrote the words down in his notebook, got the anger out of his system and promptly put it away.

Woody named his song *"God Bless America for You and Me."*

About nine years later, Woody finally recorded the song on an album released by Folkways Records. Pete Seeger heard the album and noticed a curious tune with some odd lyrics and he asked Woody about it. Woody explained the song was originally titled *"God Bless America for You and Me."* He also explained to Pete that just before the song was recorded, he decided to change the song's title and the tag line of the chorus to the way it was now listed on his new album.

The song didn't really impress Pete at first, but about a year later he started to sing the song for friends and to his concert audiences. Now, ol' Pete knows a good sing-along when he hears one. And he knows a good lyric too. Especially when it expounds his *"we-should-all-be-equal-sort-of-like-a-communist"* beliefs.

The song started to catch on and Pete kept on singing it. Pete felt the song could be a rallying point for everyone who believed in fairness and equality between different people and economic classes.

God Blessed America
This Land Was made For You + me
This land is your land, this land is my land
From California to the New York Island,
From the Redwood Forest, to the Gulf stream waters,
God blessed america for me.

Woody's handwritten lyrics to "This Land Is Your Land"

It could even be a theme song for their (gulp!) communist-sort-of-beliefs.

The last line of the verses, as Woody had originally written them, went: *"...God Blessed America for me."*

Woody changed the new tag line to *"...This land was made for you and me."*

Pete recorded the song on his next record and taught it to younger folksingers. Soon enough, lots of other singers recorded the song, too. The song took another 10 years to finally catch on (nearly 20 years after Woody had written it), but when it did, the song took off like a blast of lightning across the nation and the world.

Seemingly overnight, teachers had millions of children singing *This Land is Your Land* in schools and campgrounds. For a while, it was even considered by the US Senate as a possible replacement for the national anthem!

Woody Guthrie may have written it, but his failing health prevented him from steering his song across the nation's airways. By the time he died on October 3, 1967, his friend Pete Seeger and scores of other folksingers had helped present *"This Land Is Your Land,"* universally recognized as America's greatest folk song, to the world.

The first time I actually met Pete was while I was at work, three years after I had seen him perform that day on the shores of the Hudson River. I had my very first "real" job selling hot dogs...oh, excuse me, *Sabrett* hot dogs (New Yorkers are very particular about their hot dogs) from a little Subaru flat bed pickup along Main Street in Beacon, New York.

I was 17 years old.

It was a very warm, sticky day in late June.

Hot dogs weren't selling, but my dogs were hot from standing on steaming black pavement in the heat all afternoon. I was parked outside the entrance of an air conditioned Grand Union food store and I kept making excuses to run inside and cool off.

During one of my walks through the Grand Union, I strolled by the produce section. There stood a tall, skinny guy wearing jeans and a sailor's cap loading strawberries into a shopping cart. Actually, he was loading all the available strawberries the store had in stock into that cart till it was piled high.

"Ain't you that guy with the banjo...and what are you doing with all those strawberries?" I asked.

Pete stopped his loading, stuck out his hand and proceeded to tell me all about the sloop Clearwater and the Hudson River Strawberry Festival and how I should bring all my friends down to the concert along the river's shore right here in Beacon and check out the music and have some homemade strawberry shortcake that was selling so fast that they ran out of strawberries so Pete got into his old pickup truck and came out to the Grand Union to get more strawberries to make more shortcake to sell at the festival because they used the money they make from the shortcake sales to help clean up the Hudson River which I depended on for clean drinking water and if we didn't clean it up soon we would all loose the value of that beautiful old river for generations to come which is the very reason they built the wooden sloop Clearwater and did I ever happen to see it sailing down the Hudson.

Then he left.

Who-weee...!

Pete has a way of making selling hot dogs seem very uneventful.

Well, I went to that festival down by the river later that day and I listened to that music and I watched Pete sing and I had me some of the best homemade strawberry shortcake ever.

Three years later, I was a DJ in Laredo listening to The Byrds sing Pete's song, *Turn, Turn, Turn,* convinced that I, too, wanted to be a folksinger. A few months after that, I was living in Mousie spending my first quiet winter in the mountains of Appalachia.

Pete re-entered my life twice during one of those cold days.

I remember it was a Friday afternoon. I was visiting a friend in Martin, Kentucky and was walking the sidewalks of downtown, or what was left of it. Martin, about a fifteen minute drive from Mousie, was once thriving coal mining town that was struggling to stay alive like so many other little Kentucky mountain towns.

First week in Mousie

It was pretty cold, so I walked into a little Five and Dime store and came upon a bin of old vinyl records. As I sifted through the old LP's, I found an album by Pete that was released in *Germany,* of all places.

When I got home later that night, I found a small pile of magazines another friend had left on my porch earlier in the day. He had a cache of *Mother Earth News* magazines, which I really was learning to enjoy, and he dropped a few off for me to read. So, I stoked up my fireplace, poured a glass of Merlot wine, put Pete's album on my hi-tech Victrola and started to leaf through the old magazines.

Down the stack, I found an old issue with *guess who* as the cover story. Anyway, it was a pretty inspiring interview about Pete's concern for the environment, how he used music to help clean up the river...*my* river...back in New York.

As I read the article, Pete's album played and a song on the album was really grabbing me, an old Irish chestnut called *Paddy Works Upon the Railroad.* I loved the bouncy banjo arrangement and couldn't help thinking that it would make a cool rock song. This is what later became the song *Techno-Folk.*

By the time I had listened to the album a few times, completed reading the interview and finished off my bottle of wine, I was ready for a very bold decision on my part.

I wrote Pete Seeger a letter.

A *loooonnnnnnng* letter.

I told Pete all about when I first saw him in high school and how we met at the Grand Union and how I moved to the Mexican border and decided to be a folksinger while listening to *Turn, Turn, Turn* and how I was now living in Mousie, Kentucky trying to learn the music and figure out what the heck I was doing... and stuff.

I put a stamp on it, mailed it at midnight, and slept off the Merlot.

And promptly forgot about it.

Well, about a month later I hit the road to play a gig in Hartford, Connecticut. I asked a friend to stay at my place in Mousie while I was gone. While in Connecticut I stayed at a relative's house, Bill Ashe, in Vernon (Bill was a very special person to me. Of all the people I've known, he was the *only* one who said anything encouraging about my efforts to be a songwriter. He really understood and generously gave me advice and

Bill Ashe

support. He is no longer with us, and I really miss his New England laugh).

Anyway, about 10:30 one night, the phone rings. Bill answers it, puts the phone down and finds me at the other end of his house.

"Michael, Pete Seeger's on the phone," he says, and walks away.

Yeah, right.

I figured it was just a musician friend playing a goof on me.

I pick up the phone...

"...Hello?"

"Michael, this is Pete Seeger calling. I finally worked my way down a mountain of mail and I found your letter and ...."

Well, let me tell you, my friends...you could've knocked me over with a feather.

Pete received my letter, called information in Mousie, got my telephone number and called my house. The friend at my house then gave Pete the number where I was in Connecticut.

For the next 45 minutes, I talked on the phone to Pete Seeger. I couldn't believe it! And to be totally honest with you, I don't remember a single thing we spoke about. All I can remember is that Pete got my letter, tracked me down and called me in Connecticut just to offer encouragement.

For 45 minutes.

On the phone.

And on his nickel, too.

By the time I got back to Mousie, I was a granola-chomping, banjo-playing, music monster with folk juice boiling in my guitar string veins.

First thing I did was organize a tour of environmental concerts I would perform in colleges and schools, called *Earth Concerts*. For the next four and a half years, I played two and three shows a day, six days a week, in colleges, grammar and high schools, fairs, festivals and libraries. I booked and played over 2,000 concerts in six states to over 2 million people, made four albums, recorded three different songs in state capitol buildings with over 1,000 kids singing on the choruses, filmed four 35mm music videos, and wrote and collected hundreds of songs.

And I did it all by myself.

I had no manager. No agent. No nothin'.

I sang about the earth, farm families, battered women and children, water, and suicide.

Yes, suicide.

In 1987, I performed 108 concerts in twelve weeks to over 250,000 high school and college kids, singing songs related to teenage suicide. I started the project after reading about four New Jersey teenagers who had locked themselves in a car and killed themselves. The concert revolved around a song I had written called *The Passing*. After some of the shows, kids would actually dump their drugs into my hands. We even put one guy in jail for molesting his daughter. It was truly an incredible experience.

The projects and the music kept churning at lightening speed.

We brought 800 kids into the capitol of West Virginia to record the earth poem *Water of Life*, and followed it with a 28-city tour. Another 1,048 teenagers helped me turn the capitol building of

Recording the chorus to "WagonStar" with 1,048 teenagers.

In concert at fairs and festivals.   *Lots of interviews.*

2,000 "Earth Concerts" at schools, colleges and performing arts centers.

Filming the 1,481 extras for the "Techno-Folk" music video.

Kentucky into a huge recording studio to record *WagonStar,* a tribute to farm families. The music video for *Techno-Folk* was also filmed there, with 1,481 kids joining in the film shoot. Each project was followed by a concert tour of up to 100-plus shows.

Some projects took on a life of their own.

In 1989, I read a story about a homeless man who died in a stairwell one winter day, trying to keep warm. I wrote the song *Mountain* the next morning after a walk in the cold dawn, trying to feel what he felt when he died. Two months later, we filmed a video that aired on TNN, CMT and PBS. With the help of Diane Sutter, Craig Cornwell, Valerie Trimble and the folks at WTVQ-ABC, we also produced a TV special on the homeless problem which aired on Thanksgiving and Christmas day. We convinced Mayor Scotty Baesler, now a US Congressman, to spend a night on the streets and actually sleep in a homeless shelter, so he could appreciate the issue better. The night was discreetly taped as part of the TV Special, then dubbed down to VHS and sent free into 800 schools in the region. We organized the *Mountain Walking Party* which was held on a rainy Saturday morning. Over 1,500 walkers helped raise over $10,000 profit in one hour, money that we distributed to four agencies that helped the homeless.

Folk music, songs and performing ignited inside of me like a volcanic eruption and I couldn't stop.

I didn't want to.

I was using my music for everything I believed in. I had discovered a way to create a life as a folksinger in the Appalachian mountains without having to play in clubs or beer halls. Hey, no bars or lounges for me! Of course, there *are* no bars or lounges in Mousie, so I didn't have much of a choice now, did I? It was all concerts and stages from day one. I was making albums and doing interviews and traveling from town to town...and I wasn't even famous.

Nobody knew who the heck I was.

The media eventually created a nickname for me, *The Troubadour,* which I kind of liked. The term, you see, has a very appropriate and distinctive meaning. In Europe, during the middle ages, there were two kinds of singers, a minstrel and a troubadour.

A *minstrel* was an entertainer, usually performing for kings and landowners within the gates of the castle.

A *troubadour* was also a singer and musician. The difference is, a troubadour traveled from town to town singing the news to the poor people. His songs were usually *about* the kings and landowners who the minstrels were busy entertaining inside the castle walls.

Cool.

Michael Johnathon, *the Troubadour.*

It had a nice, warm folkie ring to it.

So, I created a little organization around what I was doing, called the Troubadour Project.

I used the Troubadour Project as a sort of media shield. I

didn't like the idea of singing about all these things I believed in, then having to talk about ME during interviews. It smacked of presumption, like I was performing concerts about the homeless as a career move or something. Thus, the *Troubadour Project* was created. I could talk about *it* instead of me, avoiding any chance of misunderstanding.

The Troubadour Project became my Clearwater.

Another thing I was able to do was not sell anything.

I said *not* sell anything.

Hey, how could I sing my way into somebody's heart and then reach into their wallet at the same time? I couldn't do it. After all, that's exactly what got Jim and Tammy Faye Baker into trouble.

I played to two million people in fourteen states in a little over four years, and not one single person had to buy a ticket. I'm very proud of that.

How did I manage it?

Simple.

I convinced companies like Pepsi USA, Ale-8-One, Coke and McDonald's to pay for it so the schools and colleges could get the concerts for free.

Now, a lot of the folk-nazi purists got their panties all bunched up into tight little butt-balls over this. They said I was selling out before I had anything to sell.

Baloney.

Woody Guthrie wrote some of his best songs while under the corporate sponsorship of electric cooperatives. He was even sponsored by tobacco companies for a very brief time. And what do

The audience!

35

these idiots think a record deal is, anyway? It's corporate sponsorship.
Duh.

And while they were whining and fuming over what I was
doing, I was singing every day. I was touching the very thing I saw
Pete use that afternoon with my 10th grade class on the Hudson River
shore, not so long ago. I heard the power of 1,500 people singing
together with me as I played my guitar and banjo in concert halls. I
felt the joy of getting hundreds of letters each week from people who
came to the shows and wrote to tell me how they were cleaning up
their yards and creeks, or how they were helping their neighbors.

I was using my music in a way that transcended the idea of
selling stuff, yet I sold nearly 100,000 copies of my records. But, I never
got a penny...all the money stayed inside the schools that sold them for
environmental projects.

And I was there at no cost to the audience.

As far as I was concerned, the "purist militia" could just *folk-off*.

I'm not writing *any* of this in an effort to brag or boast, either.

To the contrary, I am hoping that YOU will try to do the same
thing in YOUR hometowns.

I want you to see that there are *bigger and better things to do with
music besides trying to be famous or sell stuff.* Just get your guitar out of
that closet and start using it. It is the exclusive privilege of a
folksinger to use music for such ideals, and have this kind of artistic
and personal freedom.

You owe it to yourself to try. Every musician and singer
should experience this, at least once.

It has everything to do with the example that Pete set for me,
for you and folksingers everywhere. Sure, Pete isn't a saint and it's
virtually impossible to carry on a conversation with the guy. Pete
thinks in concepts, you know. It's like reading an encyclopedia with
no subheadings and you keep losing your place all the time.

But the man "walked the walk" and he "talked the talk". He
established a great example.

I recall, about a year after Pete called me on the phone that
night in Connecticut, I was able to perform with him at the very
Strawberry Festival in Beacon that started it all. During my set, Pete
quietly walked onto the stage and started to hum a harmony to the
song (I swear I wish I could remember which song it was, but I can't).

Later that same afternoon, after Pete performed, I was standing
with him at the side of the stage as 40 or 50 people gathered around
for autographs and to shake his hand. Among the crowd was a young
16 year old boy. I remember the boy said he was from Newburgh, a
town just across the Hudson River from Beacon.

The kid carried a poster in his hand. He managed to get Pete's
attention and proudly showed him his advertisement. It seems the
young boy fancied himself to be a folksinger, too, and got himself a gig
at a small coffeehouse. The poster had his photo and name in big
mimeographed letters, shouting out about how great he was and what

a wonderful performer he was.

Well, Pete looked at the poster, then at the 50 people waiting to see him...and excused himself from the crowd.

He took the boy and his poster to a quiet spot under a nearby tree and, for the next fifteen minutes, sat down with the kid and talked to him about the music business. He explained why the kid should tone down the wording of his poster. He told the young boy how there is no such thing as a star, that we are all just people...The same...Equal. And, as he goes through life singing his songs, he should remember that it's by far better to make *friends* than to make *fans.*

Friends last longer, Pete told him.

So, I stood off to the side and watched this wealthy, world famous man who left a crowd of admirers and media folks behind just to sit with a green, brash 16 year old kid instead.

. . . the same man who tracked down a young guy living in Mousie to offer encouragement when I said I wanted to be a folksinger.

. . . the same man who felt that music and an old wooden boat could help people try to clean up the Hudson River, and then did it.

. . . the same man who eventually found greatness in a friend's song and helped send it around the world.

Nope, I'm not going to ramble on with a bunch of emotional drivel about why Pete is the greatest human being on planet earth.

He's not.

After all, Pete *sails* down the Hudson, he doesn't *walk* on it.

But he sure is a nice guy.

Personal Note: I think it's fair to say that Pete was very influential on my career, inspirationally if not musically. My music certainly takes off in different directions from his.

But, for years, Pete traveled the world and established a unique concert habit that has lasted even till now: Pete likes the audience to sing with him. The sound of a concert hall full of voices has become a trademark of the Pete Seeger style and sound.

The last studio album Pete put out was back in the mid-seventies called *Circles and Seasons* (this is the album that had *The Garden Song, Maple Syrup Time, The Photographer* and other cool songs on it) and was produced by Fred Hellerman of The Weavers. Anyway, he put out some live albums with Arlo and some older Carnegie Hall concerts on CD, but no new studio album...until 1996 when Paul Winter (of the Paul Winter Consort), after a few years of coaxing and prodding, finally convinced Pete to go back into the studio again.

The result is a warm, brilliant work that is truly Pete not only at his best but also, I think, in his best setting. Just picture Pete Seeger singing and playing his banjo with three of the finest vocal choirs in the USA, and you will get the idea of the new CD, simply titled *Pete.*

(Contact Living Music Records, PO Box 72, Litchfield, CT 06759)

Traditional American Strawberry Shortcake

a recipe

Being known worldwide for my gastronomical prowess, I'm all the time looking for great new dishes. I first experienced this dessert along the shores of the Hudson River near Beacon, New York. It was at a concert for the environment put on by the folks that built the great Clearwater Sloop, organized and spirited by Pete Seeger, famed songwriter, folksinger, environmental wood chopper and Strawberry Shortcake King.

So, treat this recipe for what it is: a folk song you can chew.

What I mean is, go ahead and play with the recipe instructions to fit your own pallet and imagination. Like a good folk song, strawberry shortcake is really hard to screw up. *Two quarts of strawberries should do about six people, so adjust the recipe accordingly.* Like Pete says, the worst thing you can do is shortchange your guests on the shortcake, so make sure you have enough to start with.

The Sloop Clearwater

Photo by Charles Porter

For a party of 15-18 people, you will need 6 quarts of nice, ripe strawberries.

Step one:
* Slice (not mash, crush or squish) 3 quarts of strawberries
* place strawberries into a bowl
* add 1/4 cup sugar on top

Step two:
* Hull (not slice, crush, mash or squish) the other 3 quarts of strawberries
* If the berries are nice and sweet, no need for more sugar. Let ye ol' tongue decide

Step three:
Make your shortcake. Use your own recipe or knead dry:
* 2 1/2 cups of flour
* 1/2 pound of butter
* 3 teaspoons of baking powder
* 1 tablespoon of sugar
* a smidge of salt (you can define "smidge" as you see fit)

When you are about 25 minutes from serving your dessert,

Step four: * in 30 seconds, add enough milk to the kneaded flour to
make it sticky enough to push a lump off the mixing spoon
* spread the mix into your large baking pan
* bake at 350 degrees for about 15-20 minutes, or until the
shortcake is brown on top and done in the middle

Step five: * while the shortcake is baking, add 1/4 teaspoon of
vanilla and 1/4 cup of sugar to
* 2 quarts of COLD whipping cream. Whip and chill.

Now, go back and finish dinner. When you're ready (or the shortcake is finished baking, whichever comes first), do the following. Quickly. Faster than a speeding bullet.

Step six: Remove your perfectly baked, golden brown shortcake from
the oven, cut into 3" squares, slit them in half horizontally,
put a pat of butter inside, and add the sliced berries.
Put the top half of the shortbread on, add whipped cream and
toss a handful of hulled strawberries on top.

       This recipe will serve a party of 15-18 guests, assuming they're not a bunch of dessert hogs. Serve at your kitchen table with a cold glass of milk.
       Fasten your seatbelt, look both ways...and dig in!

Me and Pete chowin' down on shortcake.

Over The Mountain

Traditional words and music; originally performed by Uncle Dave Macon
Arranged and adapted by Michael Johnathon
©1995 Rachel-Aubrey Music/BMI
as performed on the CD "WoodSongs"

Banjo Tab and Chords

BANJO (CAPO 2)

Over the Mountain

I'm always lighthearted and easy
not a care in the world have I
because I'm loved by an Ollie
and I couldn't forget if I tried

She lives far away o'er the mountains
Where the little birds sing on the trees
and the cabin's all covered in ivy
and my Ollie is waiting for me

For it's over, it's over the mountains
where the little birds sing on the trees
and the cabin's all covered in ivy
and my Ollie is waiting for me

The day I bid goodbye to Ollie
Is a day I will never forget
for the tears bubbled up from their slumber
I fancy I see them yet

And they looked like the pearls on the ocean
as she wept her tales of love
and she said, "My dear boy, don't forget me
till we meet here again or above"

For it's over, it's over the mountains
where the little birds sing on the trees
and the cabin's all covered in ivy
and my Ollie is waiting for me

The great Uncle Dave Macon

Weaver and the Wood

"Every man looks at his wood pile with affection..."
Henry David Thoreau

Don West was an idealistic mountain poet. In the 1940's he built a school and community center called the Appalachian South Folklife Center in Pipestem, West Virginia. Every fall, they put together a folk festival on the side of a beautiful mountain.

Don and his artist wife, Connie have both passed on, but I've made many good friends from my nights spent around a big fire at Pipestem *(songwriters like Bill Hudson, Roger Sprung and others whom I still keep in touch with)*, singing and talking and passing a bottle of cheap wine around till 4am. I recommend that every folksinger find themselves a good festival and contribute your efforts to help keep it going. You will be surprised and enriched by the friends you make.

One couple I became especially close to is Sam and Mark Fixture, a husband and wife who lived the nomad, hippy lifestyle out of their van, going from festival to festival selling their handmade sculptures and crafts. Sam would weave beautiful cloth garments and make stained glass. Mark sculpted statues out of wood.

One night, Sam and Mark told me about their plans to build a homestead in the mountains together. The next day, I wrote this poem for them as a gift...

Poet Don West

The Weaver sits before her loom
and guides her thread of gold
her dreams are bound in tapestry
and every garment fold
Her eyes are dressed in painters love
her hands an artist's brush
when evening comes she lights the night
with candle flames of love

The Woodsman in his studio
finds magic in his wood
he carves his dreams within the oak
of a home built strong and good
In a woodwright's trance he dreams ahead
of a cabin he'll build with pride
and he strokes his beard and he carves his wood
with the Weaver at his side

Photo by Warren Brunner   Weaver and the Wood poem ©1995/Michael Johnathon/Rachel-Aubrey Music/BMI

Young & Alone

Words and Music by
Michael Johnathon
©1991 TechnoFolk Music Group/BMI
as performed on the CD "Dreams of Fire"

Drop D tuning on acoustic guitar
Played with an "attitude".

Find an emp-ty ta-ble at a small ca-fe,— Sip-pin' at your cof-fee like you

spend your day,— Just a drop at a time, 'til it goes a-way,—

And you stum-ble through your prob-lems as you look a-round,

Eve-ry-bod-y's mak-ing the ex-act same sound. Youth is a treas-ure that is

44

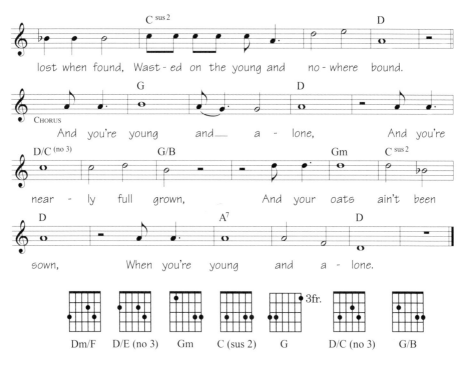

lost when found, Wast-ed on the young and no-where bound.

And you're young and___ a - lone, And you're near - ly full grown, And your oats ain't been sown, When you're young and a - lone.

Dm/F   D/E (no 3)   Gm   C (sus 2)   G   D/C (no 3)   G/B

Young & Alone

Find an empty table at a small cafe'
Sippin' at your coffee like you spend your day
Just a drop at a time, 'til it goes away
And you stumble through your problems as you
look around
Everybody's making the exact same sound
Youth is a treasure that is lost when found
Wasted on the young and nowhere bound

Cause the money you need is way too tight
You can't afford to get your credit right
You make believe everything's all right
And you're choking down your daddy's bills
The good life became a poison pill
Like a bullet through your window sill
And you're the one it's gonna kill

(Chorus)
And you're young and alone
And you're nearly full grown
And your oats ain't been sown
When you're young and alone

The job you got is really secure
And if you give your blood you can be sure

They'll walk your future right out that door
But your girlfriend wants you to stay employed
Your boss acts like he's always annoyed
Your life becomes this empty void
When you own the future someone else destroys

(Chorus)

So you can't afford to make a single mistake
That's another chance you're gonna have to take
You roll the dice each boring day
And the music is sounding all the same
The past, it's looking good again
The singer writes a new refrain
No one understands a word he sings

(Chorus)

And that waitress is looking really good
And you would take her home, if you could
But her heart is made of hard, hard, wood
And you got pockets in your underwear
That's a place to put your hands in there
You grab a little joke that you wanna share
You can hear them laughing everywhere

45

Folksinger

Photo by Danny Lyon

I love that word.

To me, the most passionate and powerful music in America today is folk music. That one word, *Folk,* absorbs generations of music and lyrical momentum that ignited change in communities, nations and musical styles.

But please don't get confused on me here.

I'm not talking about the modern cliche' of folk music, of some singer with a guitar whining away about lost ships, maidens and social ills on a stool in some dark coffeehouse. I'm talking about real *Folk* music.

The F word.

Capital F.

Most of us enjoy different kinds of music and sounds. It shouldn't really matter what it's called, or what category it's listed under, or, as they say in the music retail biz, what "bin it's in". The music is either good or bad.

Period.

Which is precisely why I like folk.

Folk is the grandmother load of music that gave birth to almost all other musical genres. They are all part of the folk family. They are all "children" born of the same seed, the same musical mother. When you really think about it and take a good clear look backwards in history, it becomes obvious that *all* of it...rock, blues, jazz, country or bluegrass...comes mostly from folk music.

Here's what I mean:

The idea of "country" music came from the southern farms and hills of America saturated with folk and old songs. The Carter Family, Hank Williams, Roy Acuff and other "originators" of the country genre took their musical cues and melodies from the folk songs that came from generations of singers before them.

Rock music, on the other hand, was born simply of folksingers "plugging in," basically. The main three-chord foundations of rock were actually born of old Negro spirituals and blues music. What made it "rock" was mostly the attitude and lyrical changes. From there, the steady dance tempo was accelerated and, once the industry started making records, it exploded worldwide as a music form. It is a wonderful example of the child, "rock", growing up and beyond the ties of the mother, "folk."

Rap music was born of folk.

Yes, I said "rap".

Think about it.

Who was the first person to popularize the idea of reciting rhymes to the steady tempo of a basic music foundation? Who's the first singer to bring to the public the idea of "speaking" rhymes to music on records?

Woody Guthrie, of course.

He did it in the 1940's with songs like *Talking Dust Bowl Blues* and others. But let's not give Woody all the credit here. People like Big Bill Broonzy and several other singers before him spoke poetry to musical rhythms in many forms, mostly talking blues, long before Woody did it. Woody learned it from them, updated it to suit his own style, and used his rare opportunity to put the sound on phonograph records, giving it to the people to decide if they liked it or not.

And they did.

One of them was a pudgy faced kid from Minnesota named Robert Zimmerman, who moved to New York when he was 19 and changed his name to Bob Dylan.

Dylan picked up the torch by copying Woody's ideas, and HE wrote a bunch of talking songs like *Talking World War III Blues, Bob*

47

Dylan's Blues, and *I Shall Be Free.* Dylan's popularity, in turn, spread the idea to others with more aggressive musical ideas. After disco emerged and died in the 70's, the kids simply fused the "talking" song style with a restructured disco dance beat, and called it Rap.

Rap, in my musical mind, is one of the most brilliant musical forms born of folk. It had the chance to be the most influential music form since rock, until it turned lyrically violent. Rap stopped speaking the mind of its artists and started to "complain" instead, mostly in violent terms. Thankfully, the brilliance of the art form surfaces every now and then in songs like *Gangsta's Paradise, The Crossroads,* and *Mr. Wendle.*

The great variety of musical offspring allows for a unique opportunity for the folk performer. We can touch each of these genres, if we choose, and still remain a folksinger. That's why folk singers really owe it to themselves to look deep and hard into the history of the music and the songs, to understand where it all comes from.

Which brings us to folk's special "breeding ground" in America.

The musical womb for this grand fertile art form in our country remains the Appalachian mountains. There is a "something" in these hills that seeded the musical yearning of untold numbers of singers and writers and artists. That's why I moved to a small Appalachian hamlet, a town of 90 or so people, called Mousie, in eastern Kentucky. I wanted to find out where the music came from. Why was it *here* that it was being born? What is it about these hills that made everyone from Hank Williams to Bela Fleck make pilgrimages to the mountains as part of their musical journeys?

Appalachia is a community of delicate contrasts. The abundant contrasts are exemplified best, I think, by the mountains themselves. Big, quiet, graceful and free but at the same time they are violently ripped apart and yet other times act like prison fences. The natural design of the mountains leave folks rather isolated from the rest of America. At the turn of the century, people from the hills in Kentucky, West Virginia, North Carolina and Tennessee still referred to those living outside of the mountains as being from *"Amerikay".* In other words, they viewed life apart from the Appalachians as being from another nation altogether.

The people who live there have come through generations of hard times by relying on their intelligence and common sense. They were alone and on their own. So they relied on themselves, their families and their communities. They developed a strong will and a brilliant sense of survival and independence. They were trained to be loyal, to love long and to let go when the time came. They were isolated, but they were together.

Now,

Art is born of isolation...

...and the isolation of the Appalachian mountains gave birth to a huge mother load of art. The poetry, artists, songs and musicians who came from those hills are legendary.

Think of it:

Bill Monroe and the birth of Bluegrass music is from there....the Carter Family and the birth of Country music is from there...the simple balladry of Jean Ritchie and John Jacob Niles, the poetry of James Still, Don West, Jesse Stuart and scores of other great American artists are from there. In east Kentucky alone, if you drive along HiWay 23 from Pikeville to Ashland, Kentucky you will pass through the hometowns of Dwight Yoakum, Loretta Lynn, Jean Ritchie, Patty Loveless, Ricky Skaggs, Keith Whitley, Gary Stewart, Crystal Gale, Tom T. Hall, Billy Ray Cyrus, and others.

Hylo Brown

What is especially exciting about this area, to me, is that the great but virtually unknown Hylo Brown is from there, too. In the 50's and 60's, Hylo put out several folk and bluegrass records and had a good deal of success. He had a radio show on WSIP in Paintsville, a record deal with Capitol Records, and a real unusual voice. As a matter of fact, he got his nickname from his voice (the fact that he could sing "High" and "Low"...*Hylo*). What was special about Hylo was that he was among the very first to add electric guitars and drums to traditional bluegrass. Pretty inventive, especially when you realize Hylo was once one of Bill Monroe's Bluegrass Boys.

It was the very isolation of the mountain lifestyle that helped all of these artists, and thousands of others, develop the muses of their songs and music styles. The sweet solitude of the mountain mornings, the crime free peacefulness of the hills, the "we're-all-in-this-together" struggles that they shared all contributed to the musical changes that occurred through the years.

That isolation also helped shield them from the electronic media onslaught that the rest of the nation endured, especially in the 1950's and 60's. That is the single most important reason so much originality came from the artists of Appalachia. They were left to their own creative flow, so they weren't copying what was on TV all the time. Music was a people-to-people experience, not a speaker-to-people thing. Get it? I'm not saying radio and TV wasn't there. They were. Appalachia just wasn't exposed to the massive torrent of electronic media that bombarded the rest of the country. Most folks could receive one, maybe two TV channels at the most. The mountains broke up most radio signals. Usually, only strong regional stations like WSGS in Hazard or AM super stations like WSM in Nashville could get through, even then only at night, to rain their signals down upon the listening people of the mountains.

These musical seeds would drop upon the quietness of Appalachia, and the people picked up their mandolins and guitars and banjos and fiddles and dulcimers and grew something else with them. They brought their music and songs forward through time, unencumbered by categories or retail bins. They played what they felt, when they felt it and with the instruments they had. If they didn't have one, they made one. If they couldn't make one, they sang the song instead.

Appalachian families and friends making their own homemade music.

Man, I'd give *anything* to experience that purity and freedom!

But acknowledgement of that purity and freedom is what makes me point out what I must say next:

The *real* tradition of folk music is that *it has no tradition.*

The true progression of folk is to change into something else. To grow and move and alter itself into something new. Real art is not static. It does not freeze. It does not stay put. Real folk music is NOTHING like the cliche' it has become since it turned popular in the sixties, but I'll get to that later.

Folk music, in other words, is the original form of alternative music. Folk music, for generations, *never* stayed the same. It would change from singer to singer, song to song, town to town.

The tradition of its chameleon styles is why so many people get into goofy arguments about "what is folk music" and make the mistake of trying to define it.

Because there *is* no definition.

A folk*singer*, on the other hand, is simply an artist whose music represents the mother load. We can play the blues, rock, country or bluegrass, solo or with a band, and *still* be a folksinger. By its very nature, "folk" as a music form is undefinable. The children can be defined, but not the mother.

Folk music was, is and always will be the vanguard of change from one musical style to the next. That's why it's so exciting for me to be a part of it. That's why it's so interesting to absorb and learn about. Folk is so old that it will always be new.

With that said, I also feel that folk should have the same artistic rights afforded to its children.

For example:

Country music can be Hank Williams singing alone in a honkytonk or Garth Brooks in an arena. Rock can be a three piece band like The Police or a huge stadium show with Pink Floyd. Classical music can be Yo Yo Ma alone on stage with just his cello or the large scale concerts of The Boston Pops.

So, why is folk relegated to an image of just a singer in a coffeehouse?

Who on earth came up with that idea? Why did that image become the public "rule of thumb" for the greatest music form on earth? I mean, it's certainly fine if that is what the artist chooses. But only that? Can't folk be arena level, too?

I think so.

As a matter of fact, history cries out that it should have been like that already. In its heyday of the 1950's and early 60's, folk was building and pulsing and throbbing its way to a huge musical orgasm. Then the record companies got involved and screwed it up.

Take Bill Monroe. He was the Nirvana of his day in that he took a standard music form, altered it, and created something new and different.

Bill Monroe was *alternative*.

The Weavers were the Beatles of their time. They took old Negro folk songs, arranged them into a pop format and sold millions of records. They made traditional music sound modern and hip and happening, and the public loved it.

The Weavers were *alternative*.

Woody Guthrie, who also would have been the first guy to plug in or go online if he could, was the Garth Brooks of his time *(well, maybe that's a stretch, but you get the point by now)*. His music and style helped grandfather the huge singer-songwriter movement and plowed the way for Bob Dylan, Harry Chapin, Don McLean, Joan Baez, James Taylor and a zillion others...and yes, even the Garth man.

Yep, ol' Woody was *alternative*.

Folk music was growing and screaming and bulging up until record companies saw an image of a singer alone on stage with a guitar, captured it, froze it and then filed it away in a marketing bin.

51

They made folk music so uninteresting that it fell from grace all the way to the bottom of the record industry basement.

They made folk turn limp.

To put it in another, purely modern term, record companies "OJ'd" the mother of music and left her bleeding on the sidewalk. In this case, however, she didn't die. She slowed down a bit, but she's still alive and kicking.

And why did they do this, you ask?

Simple.

The children of folk— rock, blues, country, rap and bluegrass— are by far more definable than the mother. They can be marketed easier. Folk takes a bit of understanding and education, whereas the children rely more on raw emotion and groove. The more music categories you have, the more records you can sell, the more marketing programs you can initiate, etc.

In other words, they did it for the money. Duh.

The finest example of a folksinger that I know of is Bob Dylan. Notice I said folksinger, not songwriter.

When Bob came onto the music scene, he released an album of mostly traditional songs. It didn't sell very much, but he recorded so cheaply (less than $500 per album) that Columbia let him keep making albums. With a dark but entertaining personality, youth and a really weird voice that stuck in your memory like super glue, Dylan became popular quickly. He was a folksinger that was hitting the top of the pop charts. And he wasn't the only one, of course. The Weavers, The Kingston Trio, Joan Baez, Peter Paul & Mary and others were there before him.

What made Bob different from the rest?

Because, unlike the Kingston Trio, Joan Baez and Peter Paul & Mary, he allowed his music to change. Where the others were willing to stay the same and ride the commercial wave, Bob Dylan kept true to the folk tradition. He took old melodies and added his own words, blazing and pointed and contemporary. He grew and allowed the music to turn into something else.

It happened at the Newport Folk Festival in 1965. Surrounded by thousands of adoring fans, Dylan looked at his acoustic guitar, kissed it good night and put it away.

Then he plugged in his electric guitar.

The folk purists went ballistic and many in the crowd even booed as Dylan later left the stage. He had no right trying to tamper with their precious folk music. *(Note: Although the public hammered Dylan*

Photo by David Gahr

The day Dylan nuked the folkies in 1965.

pretty hard for "plugging in," a much ignored historical fact is that Howlin' Wolf hit the Newport stage two hours earlier with electric guitars blasting and nobody batted an eyelash.)

Dylan dared to change.

But, that is what a folksinger is *supposed* to do.

Change. Grow. Create. Invent.

That's art in its finest form, and Dylan made his "mother" proud.

Dylan, the folksinger, created another folk child: "Folk-rock."

And it spawned groups like The Byrds, Buffalo Springfield, the Eagles and others. Even the Beatles and the Rolling Stones absorbed the life force of this new folkchild into their own music. It was an acoustic firestorm that burned through the next several decades in artists like Jackson Browne, the Indigo Girls, Steve Earle, Suzanne Vega, Michelle Shocked, Tracy Chapman, Beck and more.

Including me.

I hope you noticed, however, that I separated Dylan's music as a folksinger from that of a songwriter.

That's because there is a HUGE difference between the two. Here's a few examples:

Pete Seeger is a folksinger,

James Taylor is a songwriter.

Bob Dylan is a folksinger,

Tracy Chapman is a songwriter.

Bruce Springsteen is a folksinger,

John Mellencamp is a songwriter.

Odetta, Joan Baez and the group Nirvana are folksingers,

John Gorka, Patty Larkin and Greg Brown are not folksingers, they are very talented songwriters.

So, what's the difference?

And is it important?

"Abso-folkin-lutely," I reply to the latter, and here's the difference:

Picture America's music as a great, long chain. Each link on the chain is a song. The chain keeps growing through the generations, being added to with each new song written.

A *songwriter* is someone who keeps adding new links to the chain.

A *folksinger,* by contrast, while writing new links of their own into the chain, will also reach backward, grab some links from the past, and bring them forward within the body of their work.

A folksinger carries history into the future by adding songs from the past into work they will perform tomorrow. *How* they play it isn't the point. It doesn't matter if it's just them and their acoustic guitar or as a popular band, like Nirvana (Kurt Cobain sang one of the most moving renditions of *In The Pines* that I've ever heard).

Michael Johnathon is a folksinger who happens to write a lot of his own songs. But I can't begin to describe the pride I feel being part of this folk tradition, to play a two hundred year old Irish ballad to an audience of five thousand. Or to be part of the changing shape a song will take as it moves through my generation.

The *non-tradition* tradition of folk is downright intoxicating to me. And it has as many personalities as the part of the world it comes from.

I vividly recall the angst I felt when I recorded my first big-budget album, *Dreams of Fire.* It was all original songs, but I desperately wanted to have at least one that carried on that folk tradition. So, we took the old Irish chestnut *Paddy Works Upon the Railroad* (that song I heard late that night in Mousie), added a rock band and 61 piece symphony to the sound of my long neck banjo, and turned it into *Techno-Folk.* This is exactly the same creative process used by Woody Guthrie when he took an old song and gave us *This Land Is Your Land,* or how Dylan took an old ballad sung by Jean Ritchie called *Fair Nottamun Town* and gave us contemporary songs like *Masters of War*...sans the symphony, of course.

Musical theft is actually the very essence of the folk process. Borrowing melodies from the past and altering them into a new form is folk in its purest form. It's been going on for centuries, long before copyright laws, attorneys and publishers interfered with this sacred process in order to protect commissions and royalties.

It's part of the unstoppable changing personality of folk music...the act of passing the melody and lyrics of an old song from one generation to another, often in a new or modified form.

And that's the very essence of what it means to be a folksinger.

> *"Aw, he just stole from me, but I steal from everybody.*
> *Why, I'm the biggest song stealer there ever was..."*
> Woody Guthrie, 1941

FOLK JOKES:

Why don't folksingers play the piano?
Because they don't know where to put the capo.

How many folksingers does it take to screw in a lightbulb?
Five...One screws in the bulb and the other four sing about
how much better lightbulbs used to be.

Definition of an optimist:
A folksinger with a pager.

What is the difference between a puppy and a folksinger?
The puppy stops whining after six months.

What do you call a folksinger with no girlfriend?
Homeless.

What's the difference between a banjo and an onion?
Nobody cries when you chop up a banjo.

The definition of "perfect pitch"
Something that happens when you toss an accordian in a dumpster
and it lands on a banjo.

What's the difference between a banjo and a Harley?
You can tune a Harley.

How can you tell the difference between a dead snake
and a dead folksinger in the middle of the road?
There are skid marks in front of the snake.

from Utah Phillips, retired world traveler:
How do you end up with a million dollars as a folksinger?
Start with two million.

Why did the folksinger stare at the orange juice carton?
Because it said "concentrate."

Old Timey Mountain Recipes

That You'd Never In A Million Years Ever Consider Cookin' or Eatin'

*Real recipes taken word for word from Mrs. Fergusen's
1976 4th grade class cookbook, from a school in Cattletsburg, Kentucky.*

Opossum

Trap 'possum and feed it on milk and bread for ten days before killing. Clean but do not skin. Immerse the unskinned animal in water just below the boiling point. Test frequently by plucking the hair out. When it slips out readily, remove the possum from the water and scrape. While scraping, repeatedly pour cool water over the surface of the animal. Remove small red glands in small of back and under each foreleg between the shoulder and the rib. Parboil and roast.

Serve with turnip greens and baked sweet potatoes.

James Rowlett, 4th grade

Squirrel

Kill, skin and cut up a squirrel. After soaking the squirrel long enough to get the blood out, cut it into pieces and roll the pieces in flour, salt and pepper. Fry until tender and brown. If the squirrel is old, you may want to boil it in water containing sage to take out the wild taste.

John Estes, 4th grade

Leather Britches Beans

String tender green beans. Fill a long needle with a long, strong thread. Push the needle through the center of the bean, pushing the beans together at the end of the thread, filling from knot end to the needle. Hang up the string in the warm air, but not in the direct sunlight. Put out after the dew dries off and take in before the dew falls. Put the beans out until they become dry. Store in bag until ready to use.

To cook the beans, remove the thread and put the beans into a pan of water to soak overnight. The next day drain that water off and fill the pan again with new water. Add a good sized hunk of salt pork and cook all morning.

Levi Lawson, 4th grade

Elephant Stew

Cut medium sized elephant into bite sized pieces. This should take about two months. Add brown gravy and cook over a kerosene fire about four weeks at 465 degrees. This will serve 3,800 people. If more are expected, two rabbits may be added; but only do this if absolutely necessary as most people do not like to find any hare in their stew.

Sue Duffy, 4th grade

Recipes provided by Mrs. Jeanne Stewart, Ashland, Kentucky

Troubadour

a poem by Loretta Sawyer

Alone with his guitar
or banjo in his hands
His music a soul companion
as he travels through the land

He sings of life and earth,
of love and so much more
His voice will rise among the clouds
where the eagles soar

He learns traditions
old and new
And he's read more
than a page or two

A Troubadour of Folk is he
A man of hope
and spirit free...

(Up, Down) The Mousie HiWay

Words and music by Michael Johnathon
©1989/1995 Rachel-Aubrey Music/BMI
as performed on the CD "WoodSongs"

This is a bouncy, fun, "barn dance" song I wrote while sitting on my porch one evening in Mousie. Insert your favorite song between each round. I use Redwing, Cripple Creek, Old Joe Clark and others. Standard G tuning on the banjo. Have fun!

Banjo Tab and Chords

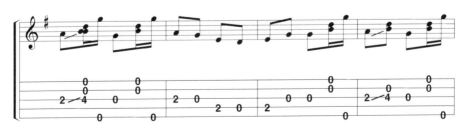

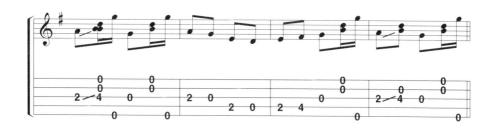

Up and down the Mou - sie Hi - Way   Blue moon moun - tain here we go

Up and down the Mou - sie Hi - Way   Coun - ty line not far to go.

Up,__ down the Mou - sie Hi - Way   Sing - ing eve - ry song we know

Friend - ly peo - ple wav - ing my way   Play - ing on that ol' ban - jo.

Odetta

In 1978, a friend handed me an album by Janis Ian called *Aftertones*. It's a beautiful album of original songs, one of which grabbed me by the back of my neck, knocked me down and held me captive for weeks.

It is a song called *Hymn*.

The song, which has Emmylou Harris singing harmony with Janis, had a third voice that totally mesmerized me every time I heard it. It only happened briefly at the end of the song, but it was brilliant nonetheless. I looked on the album credits, and all that was listed on the jacket was a single name:

Odetta.

So, for the next several years, I went on a bit of a hunt to find her records. You will be doing yourself and your kids a huge favor by sitting around the hi-tech Victrola some night with Odetta's CDs playing. You are listening to American history pour through your speakers, and your kids need to know about this.

Her voice is *magic*.

Odetta was the first popular artist to use one name, long before Madonna, Prince and crew slithered along. She was the very first client of a personal manager named Albert Grossman. In the late 1950's and early 60's, Albert saw the huge folk boom looming on the horizon and he latched on to Odetta as a major talent. He soon had his other younger clients open concerts for Odetta, to give them exposure. Artists like Peter, Paul & Mary, Janis Joplin...Bob Dylan.

As Albert's roster of clients exploded on the commercial scene, Odetta remained pure to her music and her background. She sang folk and the blues in the purest voice imaginable.

She still does.

Photo by John Lee

This pure voice was recorded on dozens of albums throughout the sixties. One brilliant album was a project she recorded with Josh White, Jr. It's still one of my favorite albums in my Lp collection.

I vowed that, one day, I was gonna work with Odetta.

That day finally came in October of 1994.

My agent got a call from a dinner theatre in Ogunquit, Maine. It was a place, believe it or not, called *Jonathan's.*

"Would you care to do a concert with Odetta?" was the question posed by the owner, Jonathan West.

"Abso-folkin-lutely!" says I.

Several weeks later, my concert tour bends up into the northeast, toward the Atlantic coast north of Boston. I arrived into Ogunquit, a beautiful and quaint colonial town, and walked into the theater. There on stage, finishing up her sound check, was the most beautiful sight I've ever seen.

Odetta, wrapped in a colorful robe and wearing a white headdress. She holds her big acoustic guitar on her lap. She has a stick of incense burning, which she fastens to the head stock of her guitar. The smoke from the incense fills the spotlight shining onstage until it looks as if Odetta is an angel singing in a heavenly cloud.

Damn!

Well, we visited all afternoon. We even took a walk along the Atlantic shore, just out back behind the theatre. Before we left, the cook gave us each a cup of fresh lobster chowder to take on our stroll. Picture this if you can, I'm sitting on a wooden dock facing the Atlantic ocean with the legendary Odetta sitting next to me on a beautiful October afternoon with the mountains behind me ablaze with autumn colors, sipping on a cup of lobster chowder.

I swear, I was having a folk orgasm!

I started to sing a song I had learned in Appalachia, called *New Wood (Gone, Gonna Rise Again)*, a tune written by Si Kahn. Well, Odetta started to sing it with me.

So I said, "Odetta, we should record this together."

"OK," she says.

Six weeks later, Odetta and I are in the recording studio, laying down the duet vocals for *New Wood*. The following night, we are outside freezing together while filming the music video for the song on a mountainside farm owned by a friend of mine, Damon Farmer in Versailles, Kentucky. We worked all night, then had breakfast together at the *International House of Pancakes* in Lexington.

It's 3 am and we look like it, except for Odetta, of course. She always looks great. (Pictured on the right is recording engineer Rick Marks.)

After the CD *Assassins In The Kingdom* was released a few months later, the *New Wood* music video was shown on TNN, the Bravo Movie Channel, and was featured on CNN *(Pay attention: later on I'm going to explain why CNN is the world's biggest folk channel)*, Headline News and PBS.

So, in honor of Odetta and with thanks to Janis Ian, I offer you this recipe of the soup we had together that lovely October day in Maine.

Odetta's Lobster Chowder

a recipe

This chowder is as rich as Odetta's voice, as creamy as Odetta's eyes, and as hearty as Odetta's laugh. Here's what you need to make about seven servings:

You need two large boiling pots, plus:

1 lb of lobster	1/4 cup of all-purpose flour
1 tablespoon of real butter	1/2 cup of chopped onion
1/3 cup of chopped celery	1/4 cup of chopped carrots
2 cups of diced red potatoes	1 teaspoon salt
1/8 teaspoon of pepper	16 oz. of frozen whole kernel corn
1/2 teaspoon of Tabasco sauce	4 cups of whole or 2% milk

7 tablespoons of chopped green onions (*the green part only*)

STEP ONE: In pot #1, boil up some water and cook the lobster. The lobster is best fresh, but the frozen kind will work, too. Make sure the label says it is *real* lobster, and NOT *imitation* lobster. After a few minutes, or when the lobster is cooked, drain all the water into a large bowl, and place the cooked lobster aside for the time being.

STEP TWO: Put the flour into another large bowl, then add the hot lobster water a little at a time, whisking the contents the whole time until it is thoroughly blended.

STEP THREE: In a large soup pot (pot #2) melt the butter over medium heat. Add the onion, celery and carrots. Sauté for 5 minutes.

STEP FOUR: Add milk and diced potatoes to pot #2 and bring the mixture to a simmer. Cover and cook for 10 minutes.

STEP FIVE: Add the corn. Cover and cook for 5 minutes.

STEP SIX: Add the lobster, salt, pepper and hot sauce. Leave the cover OFF and let simmer for 6 minutes.

Now, set your table nice and pretty. Use real soup bowls, the hand-thrown clay kind if you got 'em. Ladle the soup into the bowls, sprinkle some of the chopped green onions on top, and add a dash of fresh ground pepper.

Served best with sea crackers or fresh sour dough bread. And don't you *dare* even attempt this without playing one of Odetta's records on the hi-tech Victrola!

Oceans of Time

Words and Music by
Michael Johnathon
©1996 Rachel-Aubrey Music/BMI

Oceans of Time

The hand I hold,
the Love I touch
the kiss that's worth lingering
The song I sing
a gift I bring
of Love worth remembering

Every night
I hold you
in my arms I pray
For Oceans of Time and One More Day

The heart I feel
soft and slow
a Ring forever keeping
The you I love
of soul and blood
the friend that I've been seeking

Every night I hold you
in my arms I pray
For Oceans of Time and One More Day

and you and I became one today
and we have angel wings to fly
and if I could have a single wish I'd pray
For Oceans of Time and One More Day

I am your friend
and I'll be true
I will never leave you
and to the end
side by side
this promise I shall give to you

that Every night I'll hold you
in my arms and pray
For Oceans of Time and One More Day

Jenny's Morning Sunshine Elixir

"The Morning,
which is the most memorable season of the day,
is the awakening hour..."
Henry David Thoreau

When Jenny wakes up in the morning, she's bright and bouncy and cheerful and energetic.

I, on the other hand, fill a 55-gallon drum with hot coffee and insert two I.V. tubes in the veins of each arm while sitting in a dark corner, shielding myself from the sun...

...like a folk version of Dracula. So, call me "Folkula . . ."

Jenny and I are different that way. She loves to dance into a kitchen flooded with bright morning sunshine, stuffing and ramming strawberries into a blender. I wake up in a dark room thinking about stuffing and ramming something, too . . . usually the blender. Waking up at the crack of dawn to the sound of ice cubes grinding away in the kitchen is not exactly pleasant. But the results are, and I encourage you to try this.

So, next time you lay in bed on a miserable, rainy Monday morning and desperately want a shot of cheap whiskey to help you face another week of mundane monetary maneuverings...

...try this instead!

In a standard kitchen blender, stuff and ram the following:

6-10 ice cubes
1/2 cup of orange juice
1/2 cup of pineapple juice
2 sliced bananas
6-10 sliced strawberries

Flip on the blender for 30 seconds and you're done!

Be sure to play some good morning music like an Alison Krauss or Tony Rice CD. Then slowly sip this elixir from a clear, wet glass as you recline on your back porch, reading the newspaper...even if it means getting up half an hour early to do it.

Nothing will help you start enjoying the day quicker than by waking up slowly!

Higher Dream

a poem for my father

Where is life lost
in this desperate pursuit of living?
Is it crushed by the weight
of our Higher Dreams?

Shall we achieve our sainthood
with no struggle
or shed the illusions of time
like fog along the distant Past?

I've studied the course
of my own so-called brilliant future
and I was blinded by the light
of my Higher Dreams.

I've pursued the unreachable
on the wings of a poet,
deceived by this folly like a
thorny crown under a veil of lace.

I was fooled by the strength of old love,
the overpowering brilliance of old love,
the unshakable vision of old love,
and the unread poems
of my Higher Dream.

Like Elliot, I spoke of the unspoken,
sang the ballads of the unsung,
kept the anger of those hated,
even described visions to those
I thought were blind.

And finally, alone with my great unknown
I feel only the slight tremors of Bliss,
the smallest wink of Heaven,
just a whisper of Love...

...all in the shadows
        of this Higher Dream.

Sexy Pasta Tomato Sauce

An Affectionate Recipe

I hate Ragu.

Pasta sauce from a jar is like listening to the Muzak version of your favorite song in an elevator while on your way to the dentist.

It's artificial and leaves you stressed.

Yes, I take my pasta sauce seriously. Almost as serious as my brand of guitar strings. Trust me when I tell you, if pasta sauce could be a beautiful, buxom blonde...then this is it, right here... Pamela Anderson in a covered pot.

So, turn the lights down low, put on something sexy, set the music down softly, and get a pan. We're gonna make sweet sauce together...

You will need:

> 32 oz. can of tomato puree, 16 oz. can of diced tomatoes, 8 oz. can of tomato paste
> 1/2 stick of real salted butter, basil (fresh if you can get it),
> parsley, real olive oil, salt,
> two cloves of fresh diced garlic, garlic powder, honey, and
> mountain burgundy wine (best you can afford) or Merlot.

Now, the wine is important. Pour a glass and drink it. This will get you in the mood. Pour a glass for your partner. This will not only get them in the mood too, but helps them not notice if this recipe doesn't work out for some reason.

Step one:
* in a good sized pot, pour about 1/8 cup of real olive oil. Don't wimp out and think using vegetable or corn oil will work just as well. *It don't.* 'nuff said.

* turn on the stove and heat up the oil. Don't let it burn or boil, just get it good and hot.

* get your garlic cloves (make sure they are diced nice and small) and put into hot oil.

Step two:
* add diced tomatoes, tomato paste and tomato puree into pan. Get an electric mixer and SLOWLY mix the contents while it heats. Add a 1/4 stick of butter.

* add 4 tablespoons of garlic powder, a tablespoon of honey and a half teaspoon of salt. Put your mixer away, get a wooden spoon and stir.

Slowly, put an arm around your partner and sway in unison to the movement of the sauce in the pan while you continue stirring. After a few minutes of tenderly teasing your lover, get the bottle of wine, and drink a swig. That's right, from the bottle, don't even bother with a glass. This makes you look worldly and "cool," two very important qualities you need to have in order to appreciate a good pasta sauce. Next,

step three:
* add 5 tablespoons or two swigs, or one good sized gulp of wine to the pot.
* add the remaining butter (1/4 stick) and several good shakes of dried parsley and the basil.

Cover and cook SLOWLY for at least an hour. If you want to ruin it by adding meat or chicken, this is the time. This is great with a thin linguini or angel hair pasta. When you cook the pasta, add a slab of butter while it is still in the drainer and mix it in good. Serve with homemade bread, a candle or two on the table, some soft, romantic music...and, Oh Yes! That mountain burgundy wine!

OK, you wanna make a pure Michael Johnathon style sauce? Just follow the above instructions to the letter (including the wine and your sweet baby), plus add the following,

* about 30 minutes before the sauce is done simmering, get a fist full of salted, hulled sunflower seeds and mix them into the pot.

* about 15 minutes before the sauce is done simmering, get two palm fulls (NOT fist fulls) of shredded mozzarella cheese and mix it into the pot. You will be amazed at how much this will thicken up a pot of sauce!

Remember: pasta sauce is like true love, it's always better the day after.

The best way to serve pasta is with this sauce and grated romano cheese on top. Don't forget the fresh bread and candles on the table. Always serve your wine in a wet wine glass and never, NEVER forget the napkins.

Of course, if your lover is sitting across the table and gets a little on the side of her mouth, you can always kiss it away...which is what makes this stuff so darn sexy!

Photo by Dan Dinescu

"Michael who?"

69

Freedom

"I believe we're on an irreversible trend toward more freedom and democracy, but that could change."
Vice President Dan Quayle, 1991

When I first wrote this song, I thought it was about apartheid and persecution in South Africa.

But it isn't.

I've since realized that it's about censorship as a whole. It's about a woman whose husband squeezes the personality right out of her. It's about a young artist trying to express their ideas and vision to a world that won't listen or see. It's about a black man living in the confines of a white world, or about being so trapped inside your own head that you can't escape.

It's about searching for the right to say "No".

When thinking about what this song means, it occurred to me that freedom has many facets. It is a delicate, precious thing. It is also an idea that is easily misunderstood.

We enjoy life in what is considered to be the most autonomous and free society in the world.

But is it really?

How free are you when you are forced to vote "Yes" all the time? Think about it...it's a good question.

For example, there are two candidates running for an office. You can only vote "yes" for one or for the other, or simply not vote. That's not much of a choice, you know.

To me, true freedom comes when you have the right to look at the choices offered and literally vote "No".

That's power of choice.

That's freedom.

One of the greatest stories in the Bible is the account of Adam in the Garden of Eden. God offered Adam choices that he could vote "Yes" for and also gave him the right to vote "No" if he so decided *(which is exactly what the idiot did)*.

It's not a foreign concept.

In the 1980's, Ronald and Nancy Reagan tried to remind young folks that they also had the right to vote "No" when offered drugs. A lot of people made fun of that "Just Say No" phrase, but I thought it was pretty smart. Change occurs when a decision is made. "No" is often a good decision, and kids were being reminded that they could, in fact, use their right to say "No".

So, why aren't adults given that right during an election? Why are grownups treated as children, unable to decide "No" for themselves?

Maybe because the right to vote "No" is *too* powerful.

It completes the cycle we need to make a real decision. Dominating men will no longer be able to control a society by forcing you to vote "Yes" for only the choices they offer you. By controlling your choices, they effectively control the vote. By controlling the vote, your vote is, in effect, worth nothing. In the Bible, God gave Adam the right to control the "vote" by allowing him to choose "No" because Adam's vote *meant* something to Him.

That tells you a lot about the God in the Bible.

When given the opportunity to pull a lever that says "No," the voter then controls the vote by assuming the right to eliminate the choices. You can say to the powers that be, *"No...this is not right. Do it again. Give me another choice."* By having the right to say "No," the *people* will actually be in total control of the final outcome. They will also be solely responsible for bad choices.

Now, I may be wrong, but if I recall my high school larnin', this is called a *democracy*.

OK, let's look at it in purely human terms:

Let's say you are a young lady ready for marriage. Your parents bring you two men that you do not like and say to you, *"You are free to choose your husband."*

Oh, really?

How free would you feel if you were forced to say "yes" in spite of the fact you liked neither? True, you have a choice...but it is somebody *else's* choice, not yours. As a free adult, you should be able to say, *"Thanks, but no thanks...I want another choice for a husband."*

Well, is it any different at election time when you are forced to say "Yes" to a choice you don't like?

You should have the right to say *"No, I don't want to enter a relationship with these candidates."* If "No" wins, then the political system must do it again and give the people another choice, hopefully a *better* one. If "No" doesn't win, at least the elected official will have a way to gauge the true feelings of the people.

Let me offer a more appropriate example:

Let's say the public, realizing that most politicians make decisions totally unencumbered by the thinking process, got real smart and said,

"Wait a second...the USA operates on the biggest and most out of

control budget on the planet. Therefore, any candidate for President should prove that they can, in fact, manage a budget. We will make political fundraising against the law for presidential contenders. They will run their campaigns on a budget provided by the taxpayers instead. This will eliminate private interests and the public will protect itself by funding fixed campaign budgets to qualifying candidates, thereby forcing them to operate on the provided budget."

Having a fixed budget, the candidates will suddenly find attacking each other too expensive, and they will stick to the issues at hand (gee, what a concept...). At election time, the public will have a chance to review the actions and results of each candidate and vote for the one they prefer. Or, they will look at the two or three who are running and say, *"No way, José...not these guys,"* and vote "No" instead of being forced to vote "Yes" for someone they believe failed as a candidate or did not prove worthy enough for their vote.

The point here is that bona fide freedom will allow "No" into the equation, whether it's in government, religion or in your family life. That way, the results of our decisions will become more manifest, more honest. That's why God let Adam vote "No", so he could test whether Adam would be truly responsible and appreciative for that beautiful garden and the life He gave him. Adam wasn't a robot, preprogrammed to do what God said. God gave Adam the gift of freedom by respecting his ability and right to make his *own* decision, even if it was the wrong one.

Of course, Adam made the wrong one...which should indicate the extent that we can trust human rule.

Look at us, after centuries upon centuries of various forms of government and what are we doing? Still fighting, still at war, still overrun with hungry, poor people. Still putting money and oil and greed first. We flow like huge ocean waves from one idea into the next, one candidate to another. We have searched for *everything* yet found nothing. One month the Republicans are the best, the next the Democrats lead in the polls. One day Ross Perot is King, the next he's the political jokerman. We cloak stagnant ideas in glorious robes of change and call it "new," but it isn't. It's the same thing over and over again.

No wonder so many folks are fed up and cynical.

And the result?

We have become our own worst enemy.

It used to be that we could identify our enemies in other lands. Once upon a time, they were apart from us and lived away from us.

Now, they *are* us.

We are the ones blowing up our federal buildings. *We* are the ones sending explosives through the mail to make political statements. *We* are the ones splintering our society into little fringe groups called "militia freedom fighters."

Freedom fighters?

Now, there's a scary bunch. These militia dudes are basically a bunch of paranoid military wanna-be's who want to *force* you to be free.

Go figure.

But they aren't free.

And their ideas won't give birth to freedom.

Because true freedom is not paranoid. True freedom does not fear "No." True freedom views "No" as a powerful statement of its right to exist.

'course, it's just a folksinger's opinion.

"I well know that to earthling man his way does not belong.
It does not belong to man who is walking
even to direct his own step..."
prophet Jeremiah, 10:23

PERSONAL NOTE:

As for the song, *Freedom,*

I'm including it in this book because so many people have started playing it and I'm often asked for the sheet music.

I remember sitting in the guitar booth during the *Dreams of Fire* recording sessions in Nashville, next to Mark Casstevens, who played guitar with me on the record. Mark is on a ton of Nashville records, including all the Garth Brooks CDs. He's one of the best acoustic guitar players around and I felt very fortunate to be working with him.

So, we're in the glass enclosed recording booth waiting to lay the acoustic tracks of the song down, and I'm thinking about all these huge records he's been on. So I say, *"Gee, Mark...I feel rather overwhelmed here. You've been on all these big records and now I'm here next to you in a recording studio...man, I feel so unqualified."*

Well, instead of a simple *thank you,* Mark turns to me and says *"Don't worry, Michael...I can play as bad as you and nobody will notice."* The engineer immediately turns on the green light, the recording machines start spinning, and what happened next is exactly what's on the CD.

One take. Done.

Freedom is a good song to sing and a fun song to play. It's very guitar oriented, which I like. The day we recorded the song, Mark turned me into a better guitar player.

I'm just glad I didn't screw the song up on the first take.

Of course, when the engineer pressed the "record" button I could've voted *"no"* I s'pose.

Freedom

Words and Music by
Michael Johnathon

Place your bars upon my freedom
Build your walls around my home
Wrap a chain around the living
And I will always dream

Take the book that I am reading
Burn the pages of my soul
Steal the music I am singing
And I will always dream

Cut the pinions from an eagle
You only sacrifice the wing
I believe we have a right to be
Always free to dream

There is freedom in a heartbeat
You can never lock away
And it is stronger than this prison
You're building in my way

So it'll attack your brain like thunder
And will explode behind your eyes
And the incredible weight of nothing at all
Is what you leave behind

Cut the pinions from an eagle
You only sacrifice the wing
You are worse than any nightmare
I could ever dream

74

The Refrigerator

"The woods are full of wardens..."
Jack Kerouac

After I graduated from high school in upstate New York, I moved to the Mexican border to start a radio gig in Laredo, Texas.

There is nothing on earth more dangerous than a nervous, nineteen year old DJ who's recently crossed cultures. And trust me, going from upstate New York to the Mexican border in south Texas is indeed crossing cultures. On the air, I had all the etiquette of a bull in a china shop at first. I was making mistakes left and right, mostly in a desperate attempt to "fit in." My problem was that I was still so geeky that I didn't realize my faux pas until it was way too late.

Yes, this is really me. . . 2am on the air at the KLAR studios in Laredo, Texas.

Like Appalachia, south Texas along the Mexican border has its own diverse culture with a rainbow of contrasts. Where east Kentucky culture is shaped by the mountains, Laredo is in the center of a desert basin. As far as you can see, it's flat. I'm talking flatter than your twelve year old sister. Which makes trying to drive 55 MPH on Texas hiways virtually impossible. Texans are famous for cruising 100 miles per hour or faster without blinking. This is mainly because of the tremendous distances between towns, tied together by long flat black highways so hot that they look wet as you drive over them.

The people along the border are as sweet and humble as could be. It isn't uncommon to stroll down a road in Laredo, passing small homes and shanties just to come upon a big mansion stuck in the middle of it all. Poor and rich, white and Spanish...and me. All mixed up together like a big, hot breakfast omelette.

Folks in this area also have an uncanny ability to speak two languages...at once. They call it TexMex, and the habit would keep me completely confused all the time. They would actually merge the Spanish and English languages together. I mean, a guy would be searching for his pickup in a parking lot somewhere and he would say something like: *"Donde esta my truck?"*

Being on the radio in that dual-language town was quite an experience. One of the stations I worked for had as diverse a music playlist as I've ever experienced, before or since. We would play a popular old Perry Como hit, then a Donna Summer disco record, followed by a Henry Mancini instrumental, followed by a John Denver song, followed by a José José record from Mexico.

The funniest thing that ever happened to me in that town occurred while I was on the air working at my first radio station, KLAR. And the only reason it happened at all, as I said before, was because I was a geeky kid trying too hard to fit in.

You see, ever since I had moved into town, I kept hearing one certain verbal expression over and over. A housewife would be surprised by a sudden breeze that would blow her laundry off a clothesline, and she would say *"Chinga!"* A young boy would stub his toe or bang his knee, he would say *"Chinga!"* A worker would hit his thumb with a hammer and yell, *"Chinga!"*

This term was so common, and used in such a broad, general way, I figured it must be similar to saying "gosh" or "rats" or "Oh, brother" and expressions like that.

You know, *"Gosh,* my clothes fell off the clothesline," etc.

So, I'm on the air one day, finishing up my board shift, the record ends, and I've got 10 seconds to fill before the network news feed.

Here's what I said,

"Well, Chinga, folks...my record is ending. This is Michael Johnathon and I'll see you again tomorrow on KLAR, Laredo...it's news time."

Pretty normal radio talk.

Except the phone lit up like a Christmas tree in December, the engineer spilled his coffee and the secretary shrieked in the outer office.

I was still in the broadcast booth sorting out my papers when the next DJ to go on the air came walking in shaking his head, followed by the general manager of the station. The GM carried a book titled *Learn to Speak Spanish* and handed it to me.

"Look up Chinga," he says.

So, I look up Chinga.

It means (and please excuse me for my literal translation here) *"f**k you"*.

Well, I couldn't believe it!

Here I am, little nervous New York boy, and I just cursed out the south Texas listening population of KLAR radio without even realizing it. I did the only thing I could do under the circumstances. I walked into the station the next day, hung my head high, and apologized on the air.

By the next week, I was working down the road for a new station, KVOZ radio. And my music education continued.

The music of the area is as colorful as the people who live there. Mariachi bands are in every restaurant and on every street corner. These are groups of strolling musicians, neighborhood groups mostly, that play traditional Mexican music with acoustic guitars, fiddles, horns and oversize acoustic bass guitar instruments. The music has a bouncy, happy feel to it. I can't help wanting to cook out every time I hear it.

That's because "cooking out" was and is a Texas passion. If I'm not mistaken, I believe it was actually the law in the state: you couldn't live there unless you knew how to grill fajitas on a mesquite wood fire. Violators were forced to eat at McDonalds.

The main industry in the area, of course, was oil. The major by-product from all that industrial rigging and drilling, aside from jobs for thousands of local folks, was the one critical item needed to create the worlds best barbecue grill:

An empty 55 gallon metal oil drum.

One of these drums, a couple of hinges, a steel grating for a grill and a blow torch are all the tools needed to build a barbecue cooker that is guaranteed to surpass any hardware store or WalMart brand in quality, durability and effectiveness. And once built, these suckers will outlast earthquakes, tornadoes, rainstorms and rust.

Here's a not-so-fancy diagram on how to build one. It makes for a great home project, so try it and have fun! I can personally guarantee that the flavor of any steak cooked on this grill will be powerful enough to cause even a vegetarian to change gastronomic religions...

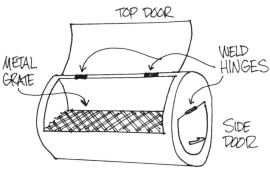

TOP DOOR

METAL GRATE

WELD HINGES

SIDE DOOR

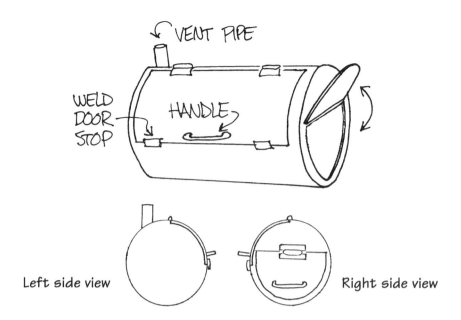

VENT PIPE

WELD
DOOR
STOP

HANDLE

Left side view   Right side view

The trick to grilling on one of these is to do it like a Texan. Preparing to cook out in Laredo was almost a spiritual experience, and they can broil a steak fit for a God. As a matter of fact, according to Texas legend, God used to live in Texas...until northerners moved in, of course.

The key to a good Texas grilled steak isn't in the meat.

No, no, no.

It's in the *wood* and *what you do to it before you cook out.* And you don't necessarily need the Texas oil drum cooker, either. Any barbecue grill with a cover will come fairly close.

You need mesquite wood chunks, mesquite wood chips, onions, the steaks (pork, ribs, fish, chicken... whatever!) and salt.

Here's what you do-

First, soak a few fist fulls of mesquite chips in a small bucket of water for about an hour. Then, clean out your grill from the previous barbecue, because a good fire needs to breath properly. Then, on the bottom of the grill build a pyramid with the mesquite wood chunks, NOT CHARCOAL. Compared to mesquite wood, charcoal *sucks*. This wood, available in plenty in south Texas, is a hard dense creation that burns hot and long. Fortunately, it's readily available in most parts of the country in plastic bags at hardware stores, etc. I'm talking about 2-3" wood chunks here, not chips. If you can't find mesquite in your area, you can substitute hickory.

Once the mesquite is lit *(this might take some time to do for the inexperienced, but worth the effort)* let the wood burn down to hot coals and spread them across the bottom of the grill.

Now, cut up some onions, skins and all, and layer the top of the hot coals with it. Just smell that hot onion steam begin to waft into the air! After that, layer the top of the onions with the soaked mesquite wood chips. Now, here comes that great smell of mesquite smoke mixing in with the onion steam. *Mmmmmm!* Once that is done, place the grill on top of the coals, and lay out the steaks and salt 'em up good.

Shut the cover, get a beer, and leave it alone for a while. The shape of the oil drum cooker allows the heat, mesquite smoke and onion steam to swirl around inside like a hot convection oven, actually cooking the steaks on both sides at once, while broiling the flavors deep into the meat. After a while, open the cover, turn the meat for another couple of minutes to quick broil the other side, and you're done.

Chinga, I get excited just thinkin' about it!

Nothing in this world is better than a mesquite grilled piece of fahitas, a hot flour tortilla, a cold Tecate' beer and a hammock about 7:30 on a summer evening!

Yeeeehhhhaaa!

One of my most vivid memories of living there was driving south on the San Antonio hiway back toward Laredo in the early evening. Laredo was in sort of a desert bowl, or shallow valley. I'd come over the crest and head toward town, driving about 80 mph through the desert on a straight road as Laredo loomed in the distance. About 5:30 or so in the afternoon, Laredo would be engulfed in a pale blue halo that ascended over the valley as the men came home from work and fired up the family wood grills. I mean, you had every grill on every block in every neighborhood going all at once! Shucks, the weather always cooperated...it was always sunny and dry. Except in the spring. You ain't seen "beautiful" until you've seen the south Texas desert after the first spring rain. The desert explodes into a tapestry of color literally overnight.

The people of the region reflect this passion in their lifestyle, their food and their music. Most folks are from humble, poor backgrounds. They work hard, laugh hard and love hard. And they cry easily.

Most importantly, they are tied by blood, brotherhood and economics to the affairs of Mexico.

Now, I'm not a politician, nor am I by nature a political person. I really don't care to be. As a folksinger, though, I'm free to observe life and comment on my musings, political or otherwise. Maybe political is not a good word for this. I'm really talking about a sense of humanity and welfare. If that's political, then so be it. Anyway, one night, during a late radio shift in Laredo, I found my first sense of these things stirred.

You see, after the great *Chinga* episode, I was banished for a while to the late night airwaves, otherwise known as the graveyard shift. I guess the "powers that be" decided that, if I stumbled onto any new curse words while on the air, it was better to risk offending the small, rather obnoxious late night listeners than the more proper daytime listenership, made up of many business owners who the station sold air time to.

Folks in south Texas are very forgiving, however, especially to outsiders who admit they're an idiot... like I did. So, they gave me a nickname, "El Weddo," which means The Blondie, or, more literally, The Honky.

During a newscast that night, I sat dumbfounded listening to the news director as he read on-air the story of a Mexican family found dead in the trunk of a car in the middle of the south Texas desert. It was a family of four very poor people from Mexico, who crossed the border and hitched a ride into America, heading to Dallas to find work. Evidently, the car stalled and the driver left the family locked in the trunk, hiding from the border patrol, while he went to get help. The police found the car several hours later in the middle of the hot, summer afternoon, opened the trunk and discovered the steaming, lifeless bodies of a husband, the mother and two infants.

Well, I was shocked and it broke my heart.

I started to ask some questions, and learned that what happened to that family was certainly not uncommon. People who cross the border are usually poor folks who are just trying to feed their families by coming to America for work. There is a nickname for them...*wetbacks.* The United States Border Patrol's job is to prevent these people from crossing the border, and I know for a fact that these professional men and women do a good job and try to be as humane as possible. The majority of these Mexican "wetbacks" are just scared men who have only the shirt on their backs, wet or otherwise. They aren't armed, they aren't dangerous. They don't want to steal...they want to *work.*

Now, as I said, I'm not a political person, and I don't have the answers as to whether people who cross the borders into America are criminal or not. I know they are breaking the law, but I can't say they are doing anything wrong. I know that they are taking jobs from Americans, but I don't know too many Americans who want the jobs they take.

All I know is that my house was just a five minute walk from the Rio Grande river, and every night dozens of scared, mostly young poor people would swim across, trying to make it into the desert to catch the underground ride, usually a truck or a van, into a city somewhere to find work. Many of them left families behind in Mexico, where a dollar a day was a full time wage. They would escape into the USA, work at an illegal sweat shop in Houston or Galveston for five dollars a day, keep three bucks to live on and mail two back to their families in Mexico.

Well, it seemed to me that the best solution was for Mexico to put its own affairs in order so poor people didn't *want* or *need* to come to America.

But I had no control over that.

It didn't help the seventeen year old Mexican boy, gone from

80

home for the first time in his life, who roamed past my front door late at night on his way through the desert. I figured, "You know, I can't solve the problem, but I can help that kid...".

So, I bought an old refrigerator and put it outside my house next to the front porch.

Up the road from me was Garcia's Tortilla Factory. They made these delightfully fresh corn and flour tortillas. Every morning the scent of the tortilla factory baking away would drive me crazy 'till I was able to get to a restaurant for breakfast. I went to old man Garcia, a very pleasant round man who would sweat a lot, as I recall.

I made a deal with him.

I told Mr. Garcia that I would mention his brand of tortillas on the air whenever I could if he would agree to drop off a few packages of fresh tortillas and put them into that refrigerator each day. I explained to him why, and he agreed. Every night, I filled a jug with water or juice and put it in the fridge with the tortillas.

Then, I called a couple of friends of mine who worked at radio stations in Monterey and Nuevo Laredo in Mexico and told them what I was doing. They, in turn, gently and quietly let the word out.

After several days, it happened.

I was in bed early one morning. It was about 4am and still dark outside. I woke to the sound of muffled talking and the jingling of the refrigerator door opening. At daybreak, I got up and went outside to check the supplies.

They were all gone.

For the next several months, a steady stream of mostly frightened, poor young men would cross the Rio Grande river, search out El Weddo's refrigerator, load up on tortillas and juice, and then head out on their night time journey across the desert.

I remember one morning, opening the door of the empty refrigerator only to find a page from a Mexican bible that someone had torn out and left behind on the shelf. It was their only way to say *"Thank you."*

I picked up that torn page and just stared at it, trying to picture the man who left it behind.

Who was he?

What was his story?

I pictured him to be a good man from deep inside Mexico's interior. He swam across the river in the middle of the night, his mind desperate to remember the instructions he was told for his journey into America to find work. Did he visualize his wife in his mind as he swam the shallow river? Did he carry a photo in his pocket of the children that he'd left behind in his little Mexican town in order to sneak into the US to earn the money he needed to feed and house them? Did the image of their little faces pull him ashore once he reached the American side? Did he ache to hold them as the desert brush pricked his skin, to tuck them into bed and kiss his wife good night?

I'm sure he did.

One of the instructions he recalled as he swam ashore was about a place nearby where he could find some food and something cool to drink. He was told it was a safe place to come, but he probably was scared out of his mind as he arrived there because of the street light not far from my property. If he was seen, would he go to jail? He had to take the chance. He could see the refrigerator outside my door, just as he had been told, so he quietly walked onto the property.

I wonder if he thought about me a bit as he opened the door and poured a glass of grape juice and filled his pockets with fresh flour tortillas. Did he wonder who I was? What I was like? He must have, because he was moved enough to leave a small *thank you* for me by tearing a page from his tiny Mexican bible and leaving it behind.

I don't know what happened to that man, and I don't know what happened to that old refrigerator after I moved away from Laredo to Mousie, Kentucky...but me and Mr. Garcia kept that sucker full every single day until the minute I left.

Southwestern Wheat Berry Pilaf

A Vegetarian's Vivacious Victuals

I'm a semi-religious vegetarian, a non-evangelical herb worshiper who will sneak in a good mesquite broiled steak now and then when the Tomato gods ain't lookin'.

Gastronomically speaking, I'm sort of like a veggie version of Jimmy Swaggart...I talk a big talk and then, when you least expect it, I turn around and grab me a piece of meat. Afterwards I sit at the table in front of a plate full of bones and tearfully cry, "Oh, Lord...I have *sinned!*"

Of course, the only thing I ever get when I pass the plate is another helping, but I do know one thing...a bowl full of this will surely make you feel *born'd agin!*

3/4 cup uncooked wheat berries	2 six-inch Anaheim chiles
1 cup diced red bell pepper	1 cup diced and peeled jicama
3/4 cup of minced red onion	1/3 cup minced fresh cilantro
3 tablespoons of fresh lime juice	2 tablespoons of real Olive Oil
1/2 teaspoon of salt	2 minced garlic cloves
1 can (15 ounce) of rinsed, drained black beans	

The morning:

STEP ONE: In a medium bowl, place wheat berries and pour in enough water to cover by 2 inches. Let stand for 8 hours. Drain.

The evening:

STEP TWO: Put wheat berries in a medium skillet; cover with another 2 inches of fresh water. Bring to a boil and then reduce heat. Cook uncovered for one hour. Drain, and set aside.

When STEP TWO is half done, do the following:

STEP THREE: Cut chiles in half lengthwise, toss away the seeds and membranes. Place chile halves (skin side up) on a foil lined baking sheet, then flatten by hand. Broil chiles for about ten minutes or until they are blackened. Place cooked chiles in a plastic bag, seal tightly and let stand for 10 minutes. Then, peel the chiles and chop them up.

STEP FOUR: Combine the chiles, wheat berries, bell pepper and everything else in a large bowl. Stir well, then cool for 20 minutes in the refrigerator.

Serve in hand thrown Mexican clay pottery while listening to a Riders In The Sky or Bob Wills CD. And don't forget the flour tortillas and iced tea!

Time

is but the stream I go a-fishin' in...

"The luxuriously rich are not simply kept comfortably warm,
but unnaturally hot; they are cooked *a la mode*...
Most luxuries and many of the so-called comforts of life are
not only *not* indispensable but absolute hindrances
to the elevation of mankind"
from Walden, by Henry David Thoreau

I regret that I am not nearly as smart, wise or intelligent as I was the day of my birth. I have found through my years that as I learn about life, as I grow older and gain in experience...I grow dumb.

And dumber.

It seems to me that the increase in my brain capacity has a direct connection with the decrease in my ability to express common sense.

You see, as an infant, I clearly understood my needs. My appreciation for what I needed was so clear to me that achieving my needs left me completely content with receiving it. My common reaction to getting what I wanted was to be...*satisfied.*

Back then, relationships were by far more important to me than things and money. My leisure time was spent truly enjoying my life, my surroundings and my people. I craved knowledge and basked in the waves of life that each day delivered. If I found I lacked what I needed, I had the sense and confidence to simply *ask* for it. I asked in whatever form my abilities at the time allowed. I let my needs be known with no reservation. I didn't fear rejection, didn't understand barter, and I was always grateful.

During infancy we are wrapped in a warm tapestry of brilliant confidence. We hurt no one, and, in turn, we are rewarded with a good conscience that lines our slumber like a velvet blanket. By the time I hit my twenties, I lost my ability to clearly sense what I *needed.* Instead, I began to focus on what I *wanted.* Since what we want rarely has anything to do with what we need, I began to get restless.

Instead of allowing life to drift gently by, sailing upon its natural currents, I began to force life to flow in opposing directions, trying to achieve what I wanted instead of accepting what life offered.

As I lost my sense of what I needed, I also lost my ability to ask for it. For instance, as a baby I knew clearly when I was hungry. I knew clearly to cry. And I had every confidence that I would be fed.

Once fed, I was content.

Now, as an adult, my hunger is for darker, less defined things. And I have no idea how to ask or even pursue them. I mean, we don't just look for a job, we chase careers with huge material goals. We don't look for love, we over-pursue an image of love. And so on.

The vociferous pursuit of these things, these undefined desires that we don't fully understand, is what causes us to hurt others as we travel through life. We end up bruising our conscience in the process.

This restless groping and our eventual feeling of guilt is why so many of us, as adults, can't sleep at night. Adulthood, it seems, is the act of removing all sense of peace and contentment.

Children are unable to do this. They simply bask in the simple flow of life's movements.

As adults, our internal engines roar as we force ourselves to travel in the opposite direction of life's natural flow. To illustrate, maybe we want to be an artist, but a career as an attorney pays more. So we pursue a career that feels unnatural to our spirit. We can easily live simply, but we take on untold debt because we want bigger cars, bigger houses, nicer stuff. We don't need these things, we *want* them.

We might make enough money to live on, but we get

consumed with finding security. So we bludgeon our brains to find safe places to hide and protect the money we have as we continue to pursue more. We fret over the need to insure and protect our stuff. Our waking hours are spent in the seemingly tireless pursuit of hanging on to what we barely have instead of enjoying the things we've got.

I've seen it a hundred times.

When I lived in Laredo, it amazed me to see gorgeous mansions, beautiful stately homes with lush furnishings, occupied mainly by...*maids*. Think of how foolish that is. The owners are out busting their backs to pay for this place and the only one who actually lives there is the minimum wage housekeeper! Rich people tend to do goofy things like that. They work a lifetime to accumulate items of grandeur that are enjoyed mainly by others after they're gone.

Who's kidding who, people?

What good is having a beautiful house if you have to live at your job in order to pay for it?

Even in rest, our mental engines continue to churn and burn and deplete our energy and peace of mind. We might desperately wish to turn the engines off, but our fear of traveling downstream with only life in control overpowers us. The forces of life that molded us and cared for us at birth are no longer sufficient for us when we are adults.

As adults, we have developed the unseemly habit of fighting nature at every single turn. Our sleeping rhythm is a good example. Where life would once awaken us on its own from a natural deep sleep as children, we now force ourselves awake when our bodies are not yet prepared. We shatter what peace we have with the grinding sounds of alarm clocks. We awaken annoyed with the day, even before the day has welcomed us to the banquet it has prepared.

Which brings me to that all too common question that burns inside many of us:

What am I doing with my life, and is it worth it?

Man, it goes by so quickly.

I don't see any real value in worrying about it too much, either, because it's just more precious time wasted. But, that's also the reason I have difficulty taking time off from my work. I have this internal need to *not* rest, to have four or five projects humming all the time. I feel like if I'm not running on the edge of the cliff all the time, I'm somehow missing out on pieces of life that will be gone forever.

As I write this book, I am also writing songs for the next album, promoting the one (actually two) that was just released, organizing an ongoing Appalachian concert series in three cities, preparing to leave for several concert dates, working on the *Miracle On Caney Creek* motion picture, plus tending to my kids, home, friends, relationships and more. Oh yeah...and interviews. Lots of interviews.

Thankfully I absolutely love it all...

Still, the hardest thing in the world for me to do is to just rest. Turn it all off and simply enjoy where I am right now.

But the present scares me for some reason. When I was a baby, the present was all I knew...and I was very happy to be in it all the time. Somewhere along my life, as I grew older, I lost the confidence that I needed to just *Stop.*

Maybe it's the nature of adulthood.

Adults loose the ability to linger in time. We all stand at the crossroads of two great eternities, the Past and the Future. The point between the two is a moment in time we know as the Present. A wise person, I believe, will linger at the crossroads, enjoy the moment and not be in such a foolish hurry to ramble down that road in a frantic rush to pursue its unseen end.

The wisest moment of my life, I believe, was when I was too young to realize I didn't know what I was missing.

"On the plains of hesitation lay the bones of countless millions
Who, as the dawn of victory approached, lay down to rest
And while resting,
died."

Anonymous

A sign posted over my ex-manager's desk in his New York office:

Artist (är-t≤st) *n. Abbr. Art.*

1. One who is able by virtue of imagination and talent to create works of aesthetic value in the fine arts.
2. A person whose work shows exceptional creative ability or skill.
3. The person singing at the front of the stage for free so the rest of the band can get paid.

Walden
The Ballad of Thoreau

Words and Music by
Michael Johnathon
©1991 TechnoFolk Music Group/BMI
as performed on the CD "Dreams of Fire"

The magic of moonlight
Lovers and firelight
The wonder of all we can see
Like fawns on a hillside
And eagles at sunrise
The streams, rivers, and seas

The truth I have learned is so simple
The best things in life are free
But we're lost in a swirl of confusion and pain
Our lives are reflections of all that we gain
You count up the cost, and all that remains
Is the lovely, and the simple, and free

Like stars in the night time
And children at bedtime
And love that will move you to tears
And jokes that are funny
And whole wheat and honey
And freedom to pray without fear

The truth I have learned is so simple
The best things in life are free
But we're lost in a swirl of confusion and pain
Our lives are reflections of all that we gain
You count up the cost, and all that remains
Is the lovely, and the simple, and free

Whole Wheat Apple Bread

a recipe

Every winter, my sweet little wife gets into a bread making mood. I get into a "making" mood too, but I'm not really thinking of bread.

Anyway, she's a farm girl from western Kentucky...grew up on a dairy farm, big family, cute as a button and tough as nails. And the best bread maker I know. We got married a few years ago, and I still can't believe I haven't blown up the size of a house. Keeping your weight down when you're married to the *Queen of Calories* is tough, but I've somehow managed.

This recipe is best tried when it's snowing out. For a "manly man" like me, working outside in the crisp winter chill, chopping up some fire wood, coming inside and getting a roaring good blaze going, then having a big slice of this bread served up with some hot chocolate...man, I fall in love about a hundred times just thinking about it!

Too bad I don't have a fireplace...

Here's what you need:

>   1 large egg
>   1 cup whole wheat flour
>   1 cup all purpose flour
>   1 teaspoon baking powder
>   1 teaspoon baking soda
>   1 teaspoon of salt
>   1 teaspoon of vanilla
>   1 teaspoon of cinnamon
>   1/2 teaspoon of nutmeg
>   3/4 cup of real applesauce *(chunkier the better)*
>   1/2 cup of dark brown sugar
>   1/2 cup apple juice
>   1 tablespoon of grated orange rind *(you can eat the orange while cookin')*
>   1 tablespoon vegetable oil
>   1 egg slightly beaten
>   1/2 any kind of red apple

Step one: * heat your oven to 325 degrees and grease a bread pan

Step two: * in a bowl, mix the bread flours, the baking powder and baking soda, salt, cinnamon and nutmeg. Stir it all up.

Step three: * in another large bowl, mix up the applesauce, brown sugar, apple juice, vanilla, orange rind, oil and egg

Step four: * peel, core and "Lorena Bobbitt" the apple into eight crescent shaped slices.

Step five: * whisk half the flour mix into the applesauce mixture, till it's fairly gooey, then put the rest in.
                If you over-do this step, the bread will be too bland. Just mix it up and you will have a great, homemade texture that you can't buy in a store

Step six: * pour the mixture into the baking pan, lay the apple slices across the top, then get the brown sugar and sprinkle it across

Pop this into the oven for about an hour, just enough time to romance your wife or write a new song. Then, have a slice of homemade bread afterward instead of a nasty cigarette.

Sure makes a cold day warm, don't it?

Sweet Children Preserves

a moral recipe

Here is a moral recipe, as it was published nearly 30 years ago in a small out-of-print publication called the *Lakewood Cookery*. This old lesson has been around even longer than that, and I thought it was worth passing on. Maybe you or your kids can make a poster or greeting cards out of it and give it as gifts to your friends. Thanks to my cyber-buddy Tammy in Tucson for sending it along.

You will need,

1 large grassy field
6 children (all sizes, shapes and colors)
3 small dogs
1 deep blue sky
1 narrow brook, with pebbles
1 summer sun
1 field of flowers

Mix the children with the dogs and empty into the field, stirring constantly with flowers. Pour the brook gently over the pebbles. Cover all with the deep blue sky and warm sun. When children are well browned and happily worn out, they can be removed.

This dish is served best after setting in a cool tub, showered with hugs and kisses and tucked into bed for sweet, dreamy slumber.

Rachel Aubrey's post play bathtime.

OJ

a recipe

"The tragic lesson of guilty men walking free in this country
has not been lost on the criminal community."
Richard M. Nixon, 1971

Take a large, slightly plump orange...

...and hold it against the ground with your foot. Take a sharp single edged knife and, from behind, slice it almost all the way through.

Then stab at it a few times.

When the juice leaks all over the floor and makes a big mess, flee the scene by driving slowly down a major highway. When a neighbor happens by and asks, *"Hey, did YOU make this big mess...and who stabbed this poor orange?"*, you must quickly hire three bombastic, narcissistic, publicity-hungry lawyers. They will be referred to as "The Dream Team" because men like these only appear in nightmares.

Your overpaid attorneys will then convince your neighbors that it was IMPOSSIBLE for you to stab that orange because you were in the shower sleeping while chipping golf balls in the backyard.

Your neighbors won't believe you for some reason, mostly because, (A) you left your footprints behind on the floor by the orange, (B) you publicly threatened to cut up that orange a few times in the past, plus (C) you left some orange rind in your Bronco *(idiot!)*.

The attorneys emotionally point out to your neighbors that, frankly, they must be prejudiced against you because it's obvious they have always fancied apples anyway. Not wanting to be accused of preferring apples over oranges, they stop questioning you and let you go.

The world at large, aflame in raging indifference over your acquittal, is paralyzed by its own deafening silence. Society's reaction to this horror is to simply do...*nothing.* Except, of course, to watch Dream Team wanna-be's on TV explain why we were all so stupid to have let this happen in the first place.

As you walk away a free man, you will promise to do everything in your power to find the person who sliced open that orange and left that mess on the floor, but you spend your time selling books, videos and slicing golf balls instead.

Serve chilled.

The Accusation

Words and Music by
Michael Johnathon

©1995 Rachel-Aubrey Music/BMI
as performed on the CD "Assassins in the Kingdom"

Performed "firmly"

The Accusation

I don't have to remember you, just to know what you have done
Even my memory won't release you
You're an angry, violent, poisoned man
You hide your blindness in your hand
I wish that you were blind enough to see you

And don't you know, when you kill what you believe in
You take the words of the poet
You take the song of the singer
You take the heart of the earth in your hands

Every human on the earth can't hide from what you've done
You endanger everyone who touch you
You got twisted eyes of mangled steel
They cut like blades and they never heal
And every drop of blood you shed condemns you

And don't you know, when you kill what you believe in
You take the soul of the painter
You take the spirit of man
And the heart of the earth in your hands

(Instrumental)

Your words are violent, poison, spears
and they don't change what you've done
Your GOD-like words of wisdom won't protect you
And all those marching crowds, they call your name
In pain and blood they've bought your fame
They'll scrape you from their dreams and reject you

And don't you know, when you kill what you believe in
You take the hope of the future
You take the roots of your past
You take the heart of the earth . . . in your hands

Troubadour Lentil Pie

a recipe

This is a five layer vegetarian dish from Ireland that I think is really worth a try. This recipe is shared among many international songwriting communities, mainly 'cause it's so cheap to make...and good for you. I pillaged this procedure off singer Maura O'Connell's newsletter.

Here's what you need:

1 cup dried lentils
2 cups of mixed vegetables: carrots, peas, etc. You can buy this stuff in a single bag in the frozen food section of your grocery store.
2 cups frozen corn
1 cups chopped sweet onion
1 cup of chopped fresh mushrooms
3 large chopped tomatoes, vine ripened if you can get 'em
1/2 cup chopped bell peppers *(the big green ones)*
1 oz. chopped thyme
15 oz. can of baked beans *(not pork'n beans, you'll ruin it)*
6 large cooked, smashed potatoes
olive oil, salt, pepper, milk and butter

Now, get a rather large casserole dish, and think "layers"...

layer #1:   Cook the lentils (boil in water for about 35-45 minutes), drain and place at the bottom of the casserole dish.

layer #2:   Steam cook the vegetables to your liking, sprinkle with a teaspoon of salt, and layer on top of the lentils.

layer #3:   Saute the onions, mushrooms, tomatoes and bell peppers in a pan with a small amount of olive oil. Cook till the onions are soft, but not brown. Add the thyme and some salt and pepper. Layer away!

layer #4:   Open the baked beans and spread over top of the sauteed vegetables.

layer #5:   Add 1/2 cup of milk and a half stick of butter to the smashed potatoes. Mix till creamy. Layer the potatoes over the top of the casserole.

Place the whole dish into the oven at 350 degrees for a half hour.
Invite all your poor musician friends over for a group sing or a songwriting session. Serve this dish with a pleasant white wine.
During dinner, play Maura O'Connell, Martin Simpson, the Hothouse Flowers, Mary Black, Ralph McTell or Paul Brady music on the hi-tech Victrola.

Homer & Colista

When the opportunity to record the *WoodSongs* CD came around, the very first person I thought of to invite into the project was my friend Homer Ledford. He's a delightful fellow, very "country" and very talented. He has been performing traditional bluegrass music for several decades, playing instruments he's made himself.

Originally from Tennessee, Homer made his way into Kentucky and attended Berea College, a small school in the Appalachian foothills of central Kentucky. He made his first instrument when he was a very young man, a "hog lot" fiddle, by copying the photo of a violin in a Sears catalog.

He still plays that old, handmade fiddle to this day.

After college, he pursued his love of woodworking and became a high school woodshop teacher, all the while continuing to make instruments in his spare time. Eventually, Homer became so good that he retired from teaching to make musical instruments in his home workshop as a full-time trade.

I love the smell of Homer's basement woodshop. It has the scent of centuries lingering in the air, mixed with the fragrance of varnish and paste wax. It is a warm, old, woody smell.

If you want to treat yourself and your family to a wonderful gift, get one of Homer's handmade laptop mountain dulcimers. They are easy to tune, simple to play and sound *magnificent!* You can write to him at the address in the back of this book.

This man, a gentle, thin, six-foot-tall, string bean of a guy, has made nearly *six thousand* laptop dulcimers that have sold all over the world. He makes banjos, guitars, fiddles and his own patented instrument, called a dulcitar. His instruments have been displayed in the Smithsonian Institute; he should be cited in the *Guiness Book Of World Records* for making more than 6,000 laptop dulcimers, more than any other human on planet earth. He is an excellent musician and he has toured in America and other countries like South America, Japan and Ireland with his band, Cabin Creek.

Homer's greatest accomplishment, however, was marrying his wife Colista. She is a beautiful gem of a woman with cheerful eyes and a wonderful smile. She has cared for Homer and their kids for all these years while he labored away in his downstairs wood-shop.

I spent a lot of time at their house selecting songs and practicing the music with Homer before we recorded *WoodSongs*. Without fail, I would be there for less than an hour and Colista would break out the cookies and lemonade. We would all commence to chatting instead of playing, and Colista would be full of stories about the days when Homer tried to spark her fancy before they married.

One night, after an evening of homemade goodies and stories about Homer and Colista's courting days, I went home and found I couldn't sleep. At about two in the morning, I sat down with my guitar in the dark and wrote two songs, *Colista's Jam* and *Summer Honeymoon*.

On the recording of *Colista's Jam*, Homer plays the mandolin and fiddle, Ruth McLain Smith (of the great McLain Family Band) sings background vocals and plays the upright bass.

J.D. Crowe

The banjo you hear on *Colista's Jam* is none other than the great J.D. Crowe. We were very lucky to have this Grammy winning musician sit in with us. But even that coup didn't surpass the look on Colista's face when she found out we had named a song after her.

Homer Ledford in his basement workshop.

Colista's Kitchen Jam

from an old family recipe

Take my advice...

...bring your family out to a nearby berry farm, or a grove with blackberry bushes or strawberry plants and pick your own berries.

You gotta have fresh berries to make homemade jam. And it's a wonderful chance to let your kids feel real earth and farm soil. Let them touch what the land grows, and feel what it's like to connect with nature. For crying out loud, too many kids actually think food comes from the grocery store. Besides, nothing will enhance the flavor of any food more than a little hard work.

This is a simple, sweet country recipe that Moms and Dads and kids should make together on a Saturday morning. Then let the kids shove off to school on Monday with home packed lunches made with ingredients they helped create.

The recipe has worked well for generations in Colista Ledford's family, and I can't think of a single reason why your family won't be better off after trying this out. I can guarantee lots of laughter, smiles, and full bellies for the effort.

Oh, one more thing...

Don't be worried about calories and stuff from partaking of this jam recipe. Homer is the skinniest human I know, so it obviously hasn't hurt him none.

You can interchange the berries, like strawberries, raspberries or whatever suits your fancy. Personally, I vote for the blackberry. Just make sure you select firm ripe berries. Rinse and drain.

Measure: 3-4 cups of sugar, depending on personal taste
            6 cups of fresh berries into a pot

Put over a low heat until sugar and berries are well mixed, stirring occasionally. When the mixture is fairly consistent, continue boiling over high heat. Mash the berries once you get a good boil going.

Colista's Jam is ready when you can dip a spoon into the pot and have two or three big drops clinging on the spoon side by side. If, for some odd reason, the jam don't jell, you can still use it as a great topping on ice cream, desserts or on pancakes. Pour contents into Mason jars and chill.

And, you're done!

Best served on hot, homemade bread with me as a guest invited over for a taste test.

Dancing

FACT: Musicians can't dance.

It's true...really.
Try to think of one who can. Just *one*.
I bet you can't.
Ok, I'll help you.
The only musician on planet earth I know of who's actually a good dancer is the artist formerly known as "successful", who used to call himself Prince and who I *still* call Prince in the hope that he'll read this and get pissed off. He's a brilliant musician with some pretty incredible dancing moves. He's *good*.

And he's the only clear exception to this argument.

To effectively grasp this unimpeachable truth, we must accept the fact that there is a HUGE difference between a *singer* and a *musician*. No doubt, all the names running through your skeptical little mind as you started to think about this were *singers*, not people who actually play instruments.

You see, there's a practical reason why this fact exists.

All musicians have trained themselves to feel music in their

UPPER torso. Music goes from their heart, to their head, to their hands. The hands, in turn, are what a musician invariably will use to interpret music.

End of story.

Singers, on the other hand, are free to allow music to be translated throughout their whole body, because they don't have to focus movement through their hands.

For example,

Bruce Springsteen is a talented musician who proved clearly in his *Dancing In The Dark* music video that, well, he's a lousy dancer.

The artist formerly known as "normal", Michael Jackson, is a singer, NOT a musician. Therefore, when he's not busy scrambling back upon his crumbling, pseudo-Godlike pedestal, he's a *great* dancer.

James Brown and Janet Jackson are singers. They can dance.

Bruce Hornsby, Eric Clapton and Melissa Etheridge are musicians. They wouldn't be caught *dead* trying to dance.

Country music singers, on the other hand, can neither play an instrument or dance. And barely sing, at that. I think Nashville tosses around the term "artist" a bit too freely. Frankly, I can't think of a single country singer who's known for dancing...maybe you can, but I can't. I'm not knocking the music or the town, either, so don't get your little spurs tangled up in your western-style panties and send me nasty letters. I just can't recall ever seeing a country "artist" dance, on stage or in a music video.

The only lower torso movement I've ever seen a country musician engage in is foot-tapping, or that "squashing-bugs-on-the-stagefloor" thing that Dwight Yoakun does.

So, there it is...

Finally, to all of you energetic young ladies out there dating musicians, confused and frustrated because they won't dance with you...get over it.

I know you feel hurt.

After all, your musician partner plays the very music that lets others get up and dance, and dag-nab-it, you wanna dance too!

But, in this case, it would be like forcing a square peg through a round hole. It ain't gonna happen. Oh, I'm sure there are exceptions, but generally a musician feels music differently than a non-player. Anything but upper-torso movement in response to music becomes unnatural. Gracefully gliding across the dance floor engulfed in passionate embrace upon the waves of a song is not exactly our idea of "*movin' to da music*".

However,

Rocking back and forth on stage while playing a major 9th chord on a 1966 Rickenbacker through a vintage Vox amp...

...now THAT'S dancing!

The Room

Words and Music by
Michael Johnathon

as performed on the CD "Assassins in the Kingdom"

Drop D tuning (DADGBE)
Gently

Dm (add 9)   Dm (add ♭6, 9)   Dm (add 4, 9)   B♭6   C (add 9)

No - thing lasts for - ev - er like the sound of your per - fume,

It rum - bles through my memo - ry in si - lent shapes of

you, It cap - tures all these im - a - ges and

ghosts of long a - go And then it chains them to the

dark - ness in the shad - ows down be - low.

Eve - ry man is like a house with man - y rooms;

We hide be - hind the door we choose And hide the

keys In the shad - ows of this Room.

The Room

Nothing lasts forever like the sound of your perfume
It rumbles through my memory in silent shapes of you
It captures all these images and ghosts of long ago
And chains them to the darkness in the shadows down below

So, come along! Come along! Ye angel, fair and sweet
The nations proudly call your sons to touch their burning heat
Where flesh and stone must mingle on a bloody afternoon
Like colors on a canvas in the shadows of this Room

Every man is like a house with many rooms
We hide behind the door we choose
And hide the keys
In the shadows of this Room

Crazy visions capture all these words of yesterday
Imprisoned on a canvas when there's nothing left to say
The dust upon this artist's brush are sacred thoughts of you
Gathered in the silence in the corners of this Room

Every man is like a temple left in ruin
We hide behind the gate we choose
And hide the keys
In the shadows of this Room

A signal comes from far away reflecting in the night
It speeds across the mountains and thunders out of sight
It wings into the future far beyond this morning gloom
And dies in the darkness in the shadows of this Room

The Scandinavian Masterpiece
a recipe

I hate telling stories on my ex, but here goes . . .

I got married right out of high school. The first night in our new apartment in Fishkill, New York my new bride made our very first meal:

Peanut butter and fluff on white bread.

Fluff...you know, that white gooey marshmallow mixture in a jar. I kept my mouth shut, ate the dinner, and commenced to suggesting we have dinner at restaurants more often. With a lot of patience, laughter, and joint participation in the kitchen, she has since become one of the best cooks on planet earth.

I mean the *best!*

Here's one of her masterpieces. It's a velvety cream dish made with beef tenderloin strips served over rice. It takes about 20-30 minutes to prepare, which is about how long it takes to get a pizza delivered (*something we did a lot of before she learned how to cook like this!*).

You will need a large skillet, a medium skillet, a mixing bowl and a pot to cook rice.

STEP ONE:
> 1 teaspoon dry mustard
> 1 teaspoon dijon mustard
> 1/2 cup cold water
> pinch of sugar
> 2 tablespoons of flour
> 1 cup of heavy cream
> Mix the above in a small bowl and let stand. It takes about 20 minutes for the flavors to really develop. Set the bowl aside.

STEP TWO:
> In a another pot, start cooking some whole grain rice.

STEP THREE:
> In a medium sized skillet #1, sauté the following for three minutes:
> 1/2 lb. fresh mushrooms, thinly sliced
> 2 tablespoons of real butter
> salt and pepper to your personal taste

STEP FOUR:
> In large skillet #2, sauté the following:
> 4 tablespoons of butter
> 1 tablespoon of olive oil
> 1 lb of beef tenderloin, sliced in 1/4" thick strips about 1" long
> and 1/2" wide.

The trick to keeping any meat tender is to cook it s-l-o-w...slower than molasses going uphill in winter. So, sauté this at a medium heat, stirring the meat around constantly till it is slightly pink in the middle.

Another trick is to sauté the beef strips a few at a time.

Season with salt and fresh pepper to taste while cooking. When you've cooked all the tenderloin strips, **empty the pan onto a plate and set it aside.**

STEP FIVE:

In the same large skillet (#2) sauté the following:
3/4 cup of finely minced green onions (the white part only)
1 teaspoon of minced garlic

Sauté he above over medium heat until soft. Then add:
1/2 cup of beef stock, and boil until it is reduced by 1/3

STEP SIX:

Now, take all the above concoctions (your bowl of mustard mixture, the plate of beef strips, and the skillet of green onions) and do the following,

* Pour the cream and mustard mixture into the large skillet and
   cook over medium heat until it gets thick
* Empty your plate of cooked beef strips into the large skillet
* Empty the mushrooms from skillet #1 into skillet #2
* Add 2 tablespoons of minced dill (fresh ONLY, if you can't
   find it fresh, don't bother with it)
* Stir contents of skillet until everything is coated evenly, then
   TURN THE HEAT OFF...you don't want to overcook anything.
* Pour in the beef broth and onion mixture and stir

NOTE: If, for some reason, the contents of the skillet aren't coated by a fairly thick, creamy sauce, mix two TSP of flour and four TSP of cream into a bowl, then add to the beef broth before adding to skillet #2.

STEP SEVEN:

Taste for seasoning, maybe add a dash of fresh ground pepper.

About this time, your rice (remember STEP TWO?) should be about done. Spoon some steaming rice onto a nice looking table plate and then ladle the Scandinavian Masterpiece on top.

I'm talking about a nice plate.

If you ever use this recipe on anything other than good dishware, all the folk magic will vanish from the recipe. After all, how romantic can you possibly get with paper plates? Only real dishes and silverware will do.

And use a cloth napkin while you're at it.

It will show you care.

It will save a few trees.

It will also make your partner think you're sensitive.

Of course, we had to kill a cow and burn fossil fuels to make this, but presentation is everything, right?

Add a small slab of real butter to the rice, then ladle some of the Scandinavian Masterpiece over top of it all. Serve with a small garden salad (with olives, raisins and sunflower seeds), fresh bread and a good Zinfandel or any cheap California white wine that ain't Gallo.

Old Time Homesteader's
Strawberry Barrel

A home project for miserable city people...

Once upon a time, not so very long ago, people owned things.

We accumulated possessions of significance we later passed along to our children. It was part of our family heritage, part of our tradition. The most precious possession was the family name. The second greatest possession was the family home.

It was an integral part of the American tapestry. Our families were once rooted deep in American soil. Our music and art came from the center of our soul. Our future was anchored deep in our past. Our collective wealth was built on the bedrock strength of this tapestry.

Back then, parents didn't just hand a *name* over to their children, they handed over a legacy.

They didn't pass down IRA accounts and cash settlements, they built thriving businesses that revolved around the family name.

They didn't pass on habits or genetic traits, they handed down traditions.

As America's giant economic engines began to roar forward during the last generation, we seemed to have left behind certain simple values that would be good for us to find again. Somewhere along the the line we've lost our sense of "place".

We don't own anything anymore.

We don't live anywhere anymore. It's as if we've become a nation of economic nomads.

Think about it:

Over half of the adults in this country are products of divorced parents. Most people in America don't own their own homes. They rent their place of residence and the bank owns their cars. Most of their personal possessions are mundane in nature and purchased with credit cards. They have somehow managed to create a permanent lifestyle based upon insecure surroundings.

Something unusual happens to the human psyche when our sense of roots and home are replaced by temporary dwellings and dwindling traditions.

Like a real tree that is constantly uprooted and transplanted, we lose our ability to flourish. Our sense of inner nourishment becomes weak. Our fruit becomes smaller and less usable. Our roots become cramped inside a small pot, with no place to go.

Our vision of the future becomes as contorted as our lifestyle.

Human beings, like any plant or tree, desperately need to touch the earth, to be part of the land and the soil. It is a part of our natural being to be close to the source of our life energy. That's why she's called *Mother Earth*. When we cut ourselves off from the earth, we become spiritually and morally shackled. Those of us who cram the roots of our life into small, rented "pots" discover that, over the years, we begin to choke and become restless.

We become withered specimens of what we could have been.

People need elbow room to be happy.

They need space to be content.

They need a place to *be*.

The more we separate ourselves from tradition and remove ourselves from the earth, the less we will produce as a human race.

The more uneasy and tense we will become.

This has never been more obvious than by taking a look at America's inner cities. Our urban centers have become hard, concrete megalopolises filled with millions of "root bound" people who stuff their lives into small city apartments with little access to the land. They own *nothing*, they need *everything* and have no way of getting it.

Can you picture this?

Millions of pissed off, tense people who don't own their own homes are crammed together, thousands at a time, into gray high-rise buildings. Their quality of life descends at twice the rate of their accelerating rent. In New York, Chicago, Los Angeles and dozens of other cities across our country, millions of people live crammed together into apartment buildings like root bound plants stuffed into pots that are too small. Their only lifeline to the earth is dependent upon crumbling roads, deteriorating sewers and decaying waterlines.

Cities have become psychological powder kegs with short fuses. The tension levels from person to person, neighborhood to neighborhood, city to city have stretched to the snapping point.

Strawberry barrel illustration on the previous page from Mother Earth News. Additional illustrations by the author.

Everybody is literally one paycheck away from losing what little they have. One wrong economic move by the powers that be and millions of angry, over stressed people will plummet into the streets of America, looting what remains in search of what they never owned.

Now, that's a scary thought.

I was trying to think of a way to solve this dilemma. What could we do to ease back this ominous blanket of tension and anxiety?

Obviously, the solution has everything to do with the dissolution of the cities. Send people back to the land from whence they came, I say! Take their squeezed, impacted roots out of those small cramped pots and let them spread their toes in the warm soil of America again. Get our kids out of the 'hood and hand them a hoe (no, no...not *that* kind of ho'). Take them back from the gangs and teach them to be neighbors again, instead.

Alas, our economic system is not designed to be so forthright and practical. We *need* to keep folks unhappy, to make them restless, to keep them wanting what they do not have.

Just so we can keep selling them more stuff.

On credit, if we have too...and the cycle just continues.

So, what can city folks do, then, to counterbalance the loss of their earth-right? What can people in desperate, restricted situations do to restore their sense of land and roots?

Well, like the old saying goes:

If you can't bring Muhammad to the mountain, bring a piece of the mountain to Muhammad's apartment...

...highrise or otherwise!

Yes, it occurred to me the solution to this "urban pressure cooker" does not rest in the displacement of the masses from the cities back into the American country side. It'll never happen. Not only would urban folks not be welcome there, but the country folks are probably too smart to sell anyway.

Besides, lots of people actually *like* living in the city.

No, if being a city-living apartment dweller is your lot in life, I offer you two important solutions for you to adopt *immediately*:

a) get rid of your debt

Stop buying stuff you don't need.

Ignore what you are being sold by corporate America and lower your overhead. Make opening your wallet a rare experience. Become a financial scrooge. Be a tightwad, tighter than a virgin on her wedding night. And stop using your credit cards! Take them out of your wallet, put them in a shoe box and put the box in a really inconvenient location.

b) start bringing the outside in

Earthlings *need* the earth.

Period.

People who live in cities are separated from the earth by

massive steel and stone barriers. We have managed to create a pavement prophylactic that acts as a way to prevent life from taking seed. Concrete has become the great human condom of the twentieth century.

Concrete ruins the mood.

Concrete makes us not *feeeeeeel* life as good.

What we need is a cure for concrete.

It's called *land*.

Earth.

Soil.

We need to get you reconnected with the planet by breaking through the concrete condom and guide you back into the natural world.

And how do we do that, you ask?

Simple.

We're gonna bring the outside in and build us an old time homesteader's strawberry barrel, suitable for apartment porches, roof tops, living rooms with sunny windows or tiny backyards.

A strawberry barrel?

Yep, and we'll grow *real* strawberries, too. You'll have so many strawberries that you'll be plucking ripe red fruit into little bags and giving them to friends and neighbors as gifts six months out of the year.

Imagine that!

You live on the 16th floor of a New York high rise apartment building and you go down the hallway knocking on doors and giving your neighbors gifts of fresh, homegrown strawberries grown at your dining room window!

Or, you live in a small city duplex with no yard and you hand your neighbors jars of fresh, homemade *Colista's Jam* from strawberries grown on your own back porch!

Maybe your home is a windowless apartment in the center of a tenement building in east Los Angeles, yet you're spreading your morning toast with fresh jam, or spooning home churned strawberry ice cream into cups for your kids, or dropping a fresh berry into the champagne glass of your lover *(yeeeehah!)*...all from fruit grown on the roof of your building.

Hey, you can even do this as a group project in classrooms or at work. Just make sure you're willing to share when the crop comes in!

Yes, amid the hustle and pollution and the concrete and the pavement and the stress and worries of city life, you can still put your hands into warm earth, watch life grow and bear fruit, taste your own bounty and share with your neighbors.

All you need is a sunny location, a wooden barrel, a little hardware, some strawberry plants and about a 3 by 3 foot area of space (if you're having a little trouble locating a sunny location, then this emphasizes my point about getting out of the city!).

When we're done, you will have the equivalent of a *30' row (that's right- 30 feet!) of strawberries growing in a single barrel!*

Ok, let's get to it! First, we need our tools:

1) saber saw
2) a hammer
3) pliers
4) a hand-sized garden shovel
5) optional: a drill with a 2" hole cutter
6) some 2 inch galvanized nails.

Now, we need our stuff.

Obviously, we need a wooden barrel.

Alrighty, then... where does one find one of these here wooden barrels? Most lumber yards, feed stores *(yeah, right...in the city...),* hardware stores, Sears, garden centers, etc. Even some catalogs sell the things. A second option is to get two half-barrels and place them together.

A third option (stay with me on this) is to use a large, plastic garbage pail. It'll do the exact same thing the wooden barrel will but without the magical, rustic ambiance we're looking for.

Now, in Kentucky where I live, we have one up on all you city people. You see, they make the world's finest whiskey and bourbon out here. And guess what they use to make this precious panacea in?

You got it...*wooden barrels!*

By law, they can only use those barrels once, too.

Now, I know for a fact that in the northeast and along the west coast, wineries abound. Those folks basically do the same thing with the same kind of wooden barrels. So, I think it would make for a great family day trip to go visit one of these places, pick up a real wooden barrel and haul it back to your city dwelling.

Just think of the magnificent aroma a real charcoal whiskey barrel would add to your living room! Or the woody fragrance of a real hickory merlot vat!

Other stuff you need:
* a sheet of plastic or a large plastic garbage bag
* a perforated plastic drainage pipe, about 2/3 the length of the barrel (6" minimum, 12" maximum)
* a 50 lb. bag of lava rock or large pebbles
* enough good soil to fill the barrel
* about 25 strawberry plants
* newspaper or cloth strips
* a 4' by 2' sheet of window screen
* an 8' long 2x4
* a 2' by 2' square of 1/2" plywood

All of these supplies can be picked up at your local home center. If you pay for it on a credit card,

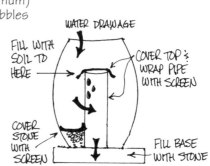

110

consider it a step backward...you owe me your first quart of strawberries as punishment!

STEP ONE: make the barrel stand:

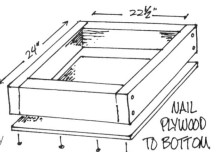

* From your 8' long 2x4, cut two pieces 24" long and two pieces 21" long. Nail together into a 2' by 2' square.
* Nail the plywood to one side.
* Line the inside of the "box" you've just made with a sheet of plastic. The plastic will help shield the floor from any soil or water. Place the box at the location where the finished barrel will be (a place like a window with full sun) and fill until level with lava rock.

STEP TWO: getting your barrel ready:

* at the center of the bottom of the barrel, cut a hole the exact diameter of your perforated drainage pipe. If your pipe is 8" across, then cut an 8" hole, etc.
* drill or cut about sixteen 2" holes

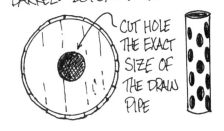

along the wall around the barrel. These holes should be placed in every other panel all the way around, and no lower than 8" from the bottom. Drill or cut the holes in the center of each wooden barrel panel.

STEP THREE: positioning the barrel:

* bring the barrel to the permanent location and rest it on top of the wooden box filled with lava rock.
* with string, tape, wire or large rubber bands, wrap the screen around the perforated drain pipe.
* insert the plastic pipe into the hole you cut out at the bottom of the barrel.
* layer about 3-5" of the bottom of the barrel with lava rock or pebbles, keeping the pipe centered as you do.

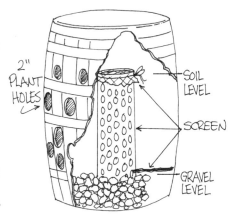

* layer the top of the rock inside the barrel with the screen
* begin filling the barrel with soil, packing firmly around the pipe as you go, keeping it level. Fill to the bottom of the first holes.

STEP FOUR: planting the strawberries:

* stick a strawberry plant into one of the 2" drilled holes from the outside of the barrel, fanning the roots over top of the soil and letting the leaves hang outside. Cover the roots with soil and pat firmly. Once the root is covered, shield the hole with newspaper or cloth (to prevent soil from pouring out) and continue filling the barrel with soil up to the next level.

* when you are at the top of the perforated pipe, stop filling the barrel with soil. Plant the remaining berry plants at the top of the barrel.

And, you're done!

If you've selected a good, sunny *outdoor* location for the barrel (such as a porch, sidewalk or roof top) be sure to keep the barrel watered until the first rain.

If you've planted *inside,* water every four days or so. Give it a good soaking, but take care not to water so much it leaks out of our pebble box and onto the floor! If the barrel is positioned next to a window, you might need to rotate the barrel in the sunshine every few days as well.

A good idea is to *consult with your local nursery on the care and feeding of your particular strawberry plants.* The important thing is to have fun with this. Share your yield with friends and neighbors. Bring the experience and the power and the poetry of planet earth inside for a change, and watch how it soothes your nerves and calms your heart.

It doesn't have to be strawberries, either.

You can grow marigolds, beans, peas...all kinds of stuff. If you have kids, make sure you let them help. I just think planting strawberries is the tastiest and most fun thing of all.

So, here you are...a city-fied cave dweller with your own real, old timey American homesteader's strawberry barrel.

Cool!

And if the day ever comes when your city collapses and chaos rules the streets below, you can just sit up in your high rise apartment spooning out some creamy homemade strawberry ice cream...

...and watch it all on CNN!

"And they will certainly build houses and live there,
and they will certainly plant vineyards and eat their fruitage,
and the work of their own hands my people shall use to the full,
and they will not toil for nothing..."
prophet Isaiah, chapter 65

CNN

*"After a good night's sleep, the news is as
indispensable as breakfast..."*

Henry David Thoreau

OK, I'll admit it...I'm a CNN junkie.

And I have been for a long while.

When I travel, and lord knows I travel a lot, I require two
things from any hotel I stay in:

Cable service with CNN and the oldest possible hotel maid.

Let's talk about CNN first.

I like CNN because it it compares very much to the tradition
of being a folksinger. Actually, I view CNN as one huge, global folk
channel.

Think about it.

Centuries ago, folksingers would travel from town to town
sharing news of the day in their songs. Folksingers were like
anchormen, really. Tom Brokaw with a banjo. That's how the news
was carried, via the singer and the songs.

Today, news is carried by satellite and cable, but it's basically
the same darn thing. So, to me, that makes Ted Turner the world's
most successful and powerful folksinger in all history. Not bad for a
guy who admittedly can't carry a tune.

But, heck, neither can Bob Dylan.

I like Ted Turner.

Never met him, of course. But I like him just the same. In
my opinion, every generation of humankind needs a brash, bigger-
than-life success story like ol' Ted.

I admire the fact that Ted achieved a global victory while
EVERYONE said he was crazy, that it couldn't be done. They said he
was weird, unbalanced, wasting his time and a nut.

Now, they call him "Sir".

Human nature is such that we are compelled to pursue the
impossible. I mean, every man asking a beautiful woman out on a
date is basically doing the exact same thing Ted was doing.

Human nature is also such that we laugh at those who reach
for dreams greater than our courage will allow us to pursue.

For example:

A guy reads in the local paper that a supermodel is going to
be in town at the grand opening of a new mall *(this, of course, is the
pinnacle of talent for most supermodels. We'll get to that later)*. He tells

his buddy that he's going to go to the mall, approach the supermodel and ask her out on a date.

What does his friend say?

"You're crazy!"

Now, ask yourself, why did his buddy say that?

He doesn't *really* think his friend is crazy, he's just jealous because he doesn't personally have the courage it would take to approach the supermodel. The only way he can compensate for his lack of courage is to reduce the bravery of his friend down to a lower level. So, he transposes "bravery" into "crazy" in order to accept his own failure.

That's exactly what happened to Ted Turner.

Ted viewed our planet as a buxom supermodel, and he asked her out. And everyone said he was crazy.

But, to the surprise of all his critics, the world said "Oh, Ted, baby...take me!" and Mr. Ted Turner ended up with the friskiest, hottest date in all human history...then he landed Jane Fonda as his wife to boot!

Having said all that, I do in fact need to point out one criticism of Ted. Although I consider him to be the most successful folksinger of all time, he is also the worst public speaker of all time. Jeesh, have you ever heard this guy talk? I've never, in all my life, heard ANYONE use the non-descriptive term *"...uhhhm..."* more than Ted Turner.

For a guy who built a global network based on clear and concise communications worth billions, he can't speak worth a dime. Which, to my way of thinking, adds to the overall charm of the guy, anyway.

Now, as for the old hotel maids...

A "grandmotherly" hotel maid is usually a happy, cheerful woman who gets her job done quickly and efficiently. They tend to smile a lot and are fairly happy at their work. I find them to be delightful, wonderful ladies.

On the other hand, a *young* hotel maid usually gets "hit on" by every lonely, road weary, lookin'-for-some-action businessman staying at the hotel. She's propositioned and bothered by each guy in every room she's servicing. By the time she gets to my room, she's a seathing, hormonally enraged, fire breathing man-hater and I end up cowering in the corner of my room until she leaves.

...and I don't blame her, either. I just can't be bothered with it.

"Hawaii has always been a very pivotal role in the Pacific.
It is in the Pacific. It is a part of the United States
that is an island that is right here."
Vice President Dan Quayle
delivering a speech in Hawaii, September 1989

114

Asparagus & Tomato Pasta Salad

a recipe with an uppity touch of class

You know, years ago it was common for poor people across America to live on a small farm in a log cabin by a mountainside stream.
Today, you gotta be pretty darn rich to live that poor.

Here's a dish that will surely raise you a few notches in the class system...no matter how poor you might be!

You will need:

2 1/2 cups diagonally sliced asparagus, about 1" long
1 1/2 cups of seashell or bow-tie pasta
1/3 cup orange juice (yes...ORANGE JUICE)
2 tablespoons of white wine vinegar   2 tablespoons of water
1 tablespoon olive oil   2 teaspoons Dijon mustard
1/4 teaspoon pepper   1/8 teaspoon salt
2 cups quartered cherry tomatoes   1 cup diced yellow bell pepper
1/2 cup thinly sliced basil leaves   1/3 cup chopped kalamata olives
1/4 cup thinly sliced green onions   2 tablespoons capers

STEP ONE: Boil the pasta till it's cooked, rinse with cool water
STEP TWO: Steam the asparagus for about 2 minutes.
STEP THREE: Get the orange juice, vinegar, water, olive oil, mustard and
                        pepper and whisk it together in a large bowl.
STEP FOUR: To that same bowl, add the pasta, the asparagus and
                        the rest of the ingredients. Toss gently until well mixed.
                        Serve chilled (not you, the pasta).

Now, pull out your best tablecloth and spread it out on the dinner table. Get your fanciest dishes and silverware. Light some candles. Use real cloth napkins. Put Mozart or Vivaldi on the stereo. Pour some chilled champagne into wet glass goblets.
The man should wear his finest tie, the woman her prettiest earrings...the rest of your poverty stricken selves should be buck naked as you dig in together for a luscious romantic repast (go ahead, look it up).
Hey... I bet ol' Ross never had *this* much fun!

Secrets in the Key of G

Words and Music by
Michael Johnathon
©1994 Rachel-Aubrey Music/BMI
as performed on the CD "Dreams of Fire"

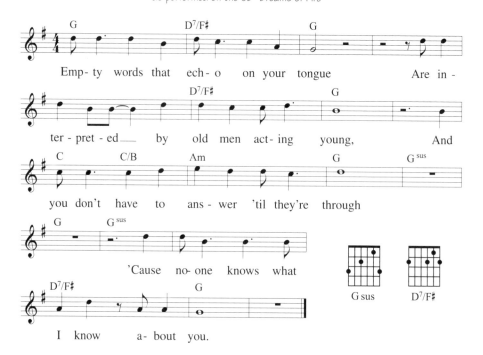

Emp- ty words that ech- o on your tongue Are in- ter- pret- ed by old men act- ing young, And you don't have to ans- wer 'til they're through 'Cause no- one knows what I know a- bout you.

G sus   D⁷/F♯

Empty words that echo on your tongue
Interpreted by old men acting young
You don't have to answer 'til they're through
'Cause no one knows what I know about you

Drunken visions fall outside your head
Speaking lies 'til you forget the words you said
Your public thinks that every song is true
But they don't know what I know about you

Fabricate all the images that you've made
Your tapestry of color soon will fade
The wrinkles that you hide are shining thru
No one knows what I know about you

There's fire in the eyes of St. Sinead
Speaking louder than the words you've never said
And the priest inside his raincoat holds his clue
Even GOD don't know what I know about you . . .

Ready, aim . . . *Play!*

The Long Neck Banjo

gen'tle'man (jen-tl-mŏn) *noun:*

1. A man of noble birth or superior social position.
2. A well-mannered and considerate man with high standards of proper behavior.
3. A man who knows how to play the banjo . . .
   . . . but doesn't

I want to write a bit about the 5 string, open back, long neck banjo and the sound, songs and music styles you can play with it.

Of course, the banjo is not my main instrument. The acoustic guitar is. Let me clarify that...a Martin D28s model acoustic guitar, to be specific. I love that instrument with a passion and protect it with my life. I have this running joke about it when I'm performing somewhere. I'll be standing backstage before sound check and go to the sound technician, point my finger at him and then toward my wife, and sternly give him this instruction:

"Here is my woman and there is my guitar....don't EVER mess with my guitar!"

But, I also *love* the sound of the banjo, especially the deeper, rounder tones of the long neck, open back Vega PS-5, which is what I play. I enjoy the challenge of using the instrument in different settings, from solo concerts to playing it with rock bands. There is a wealth of tunings, strings, straps and pickups that work best with this unusual and magnificent instrument.

First, let me tell you the story of how this unusual banjo came to be. I must pay tribute to the fellow who helped invent the instrument, the man who was first to record with it and propelled the image of the long neck banjo around the world. This is the man who influenced musicians like Roger McGuinn, Harry Chapin, Tom Chapin, Don McLean, the Kingston Trio and folksingers old and new to play the long neck exclusively.

I'm talking again, of course, about Pete Seeger.

There was a time in the early sixties when Pete was considered by most musicians of the day to be the best banjo player in the world. Of course since then, Pete's talents have certainly been outdistanced by players like Bela Fleck to Raymond McLain. But Pete did something that very few musicians, banjo or otherwise, have ever done:

He made thousands of people WANT to learn how to play.

He influenced a generation of young kids to actually go to a store and buy a musical tool to create with. During his days with the Weavers, Pete stood on stages around the world, from Carnegie Hall in New York to the Royal Albert Hall in London, singing in his tux with his long neck, open back banjo strapped across his shoulders.

Pete designed the long neck in 1944 and had it built by a craftsman named John D'Angelico in New York City. He created it because his voice couldn't handle songs sung in certain standard tunings. He reasoned, *"If only I could keeping moving down the neck, I could still play in chords I know and my voice wouldn't strain and crack so much."*

So, by taking a standard open back banjo, sawing the end of the neck off, and then affixing some extra frets, Pete had a banjo he could capo to standard G three frets up or drop on down to handle the "harder to sing" songs. He could do this without having to retune the entire instrument or play in tunings too cumbersome and unfamiliar.

In other words, Pete gave the world the long neck banjo because...well...he was *lazy.*

Around 1947, Pete was on tour with some poly-tician running for President. During long days hanging around hotel rooms, Pete began writing a simple manual about the banjo. He wrote about the history of the instrument and how to play it. He highlighted some of the great players that made the banjo popular and about the songs you can play with it. Most importantly, Pete published a homemade manual that made playing the banjo sound EASY.

Easy enough for you and me to try it.

That manual is hard to find today but is still out there in some music stores and book shops *(it's distributed by Music Sales, Inc.).* It impacted me and inspired musicians like Leo Kottke and literally thousands of novice musicians. Pete Seeger, his banjo, and that little manual traveled the globe and created a whole movement that brought America back to acoustic music during the days when Elvis was making the world scream and the Beatles were invading American airwaves.

Before long, a thing called the "Folk Boom" happened, and a

group called the Kingston Trio sold millions of albums. And, on the cover of every Kingston Trio jacket, was a long neck banjo.

So, that's the basic history.

Now, let me explain a little about my music and why I can even speak with any confidence on the subject:

I've been playing the long neck for about 10 years; played it in over 2,000 concerts, and used it on my seven album recordings.

Today, there are very few people who own a long neck banjo. There are very few people who have even *seen*, heard or played one. Actually, I'm the ONLY one I know of who has one, no less records with it. Lately, I've used it more than ever, and each new CD I put out has more tunes with it as my base instrument.

In 1993, I released an album called *Dreams of Fire*. There's a song on the CD called *Techno-Folk*. The tune was recorded with just me, my banjo, a rock band of Grammy winners and a 61-piece symphony, if you can imagine that. *Techno-Folk* was described in an Associated Press review of *Dreams of Fire* as sounding like "...*Pete Seeger with a Pink Floyd attitude...*".

But don't let that scare you off.

It's still a good song.

The point is, the tune is played all the way down the open neck. Unfortunately, the scope of that particular recording doesn't really allow for an up-close analysis of the banjo...there's a lot going on during the course of that record.

However, in April of 1995, I recorded and released another album called *Assassins In The Kingdom*. On that album, I used the sound of the long neck to record an unusual version of Bob Dylan's *Masters of War*, and on an instrumental tune recorded with a French horn quartet, called *Cosmic Banjo*, also played down the neck.

Now, *Cosmic Banjo* is worth looking into.

This tune is also performed on the CD all the way down the neck. The string tunings are eGEAB. *Cosmic Banjo* was written originally as the instrumental prelude to *Techno-Folk*. If you have both CDs, make a cassette tape of *Cosmic Banjo* followed immediately by *Techno-Folk*.

You will notice two things immediately:

a) Both songs are in the exact same tuning and performance positions, and

b) *Techno-Folk* only has two chords in it, Am and G (*Techno-Folk* is melodically based on the old Irish traditional song *Paddy Works Upon the Railroad*).

Playing both of these songs back-to-back works GREAT in concert, especially since audiences are not accustomed to the unusual sound and sight of the long neck, in a band setting no less. Both songs also lean heavily toward a rock sound, versus a country sound, which serves as another audience surprise.

Last year, I performed *Techno-Folk* live on TNN's prime time program *Music City Tonight,* and the house band went ape over the long neck. Those seasoned Nashville players had actually never seen one before. I also remember the producers kindly flashed the 1-800 mailorder number on screen and the record company got over 700 orders for the CD in just 48 hours after the show. So, I KNOW there's a healthy market for this instrument.

I also remember getting hammered with a common problem of the long neck during that live performance on TNN. By the end of *Techno-Folk*, where I finish the song as a solo banjo piece, the darn thing fell out of tune because I was playing it too hard. No big deal, but it will happen now and then.

Of course, I should have been prepared for something to go wrong that night. It was a pretty odd show to begin with. I don't mean that *Music City Tonight* was weird. It was a great show and I miss it. But on that particular night, they booked me, Mr. Long-Neck-Banjo-Folksinger, along with a huge, bearded flag-waving red-neck country singer named Charlie Daniels, who was doing a song called *"You're Worshiping the Wrong God"* (let me add that Charlie is also a brilliant guitarist, great singer and a real nice guy, too).

Then, to top it all off, they also booked Elvis Presley's daughter's future ex-sister-in-law, LaToya.

...good grief!

As for *Cosmic Banjo*, the performance lines of that tune make for a good study of the long neck and its potential for alternative settings. Tuned all the way down the neck, again in eGEAB, it allows for a rich, resonant sound. The open back of my Vega PS-5 retains a classic, traditional sound. This traditional sound is enhanced by the French horn quartet we used on the record. It turns "high octane" when the band kicks in. But you never lose the flavor or location of the banjo in the mix because of its highly definable sound. *Cosmic Banjo* also depends heavily on the performance pattern played on the open bass string, as you can see in the enclosed TAB arrangement of the song.

When figuring out the TAB, here's a playing hint:

I play the song with a thumb pick and two finger picks. I personally use Dunlop .013 finger picks. I find they are the most controllable and least likely to cause that "scraping" sound. The index finger pick is played with the curve of the pick fitted on the "meat" of the finger. The second pick on the second finger is fitted in reverse. The pick is upside down against my fingernail. This is my playing style for most songs. I will pick melody-lines and rolls with the thumb and first finger, and frail with the second finger.

At the same time.

That picking style, coupled with the unique sound of the long neck, gives *Cosmic Banjo*

Photo by James Crisp

121

its odd flavor. When performing solo, it also helps fill the concert hall with sound...it almost comes across as TWO banjos being played at once.

In January of 1996, I was able to release yet another CD called *WoodSongs*, which takes the instrument back to its traditional root. This same picking pattern is used on banjo renditions of Woody Guthrie's *Pastures of Plenty* and Uncle Dave Macon's *Over the Mountain*. Both of these songs make for EXCELLENT solo concert pieces, and I encourage you to try them. The picking pattern on *Pastures of Plenty* is one I originally heard on an old Dave Evans Lp. I really liked his rendition of the song and I re-customized the pattern with some suggestions from Bela Fleck. It's a real cool piece and audiences totally get into it when performing solo. Even so, the picks are placed on the hand exactly as in *Cosmic Banjo* and *Techno-Folk*.

As for banjo strings, I prefer using John Pierce 80/20 light gauge, extra long (set #1700L). However, you might want to use a medium gauge string of the same brand. They are bright, stay clean-sounding a long time and are affordable. I change my strings about as often as a drummer changes underwear...every fourth concert, so I go through quite a few sets in a year.

As I once said during a magazine interview, if strings could be a beautiful buxom blonde, then these are it. Heck, I even use the same brand on my Martin Guitar and I'm not even sponsored by them. They offered, but I said "no thanks". A good string is a good string. Period. So, take my recommendation as an honest preference based on experience. If you are not good at tuning or you have a banjo that tends to fall out of tune, medium gauge might be a safer way to go.

Two more pointers: Straps and capos.

The best place to secure a strap on the long neck is NOT both ends on the pot. Secure one side on the bottom of the pot behind the saddle. Secure the second end on the NECK, on or about the 15th fret from the tuning pegs. This will help you balance the instrument when playing. I screwed an eye hook into the neck and clipped the strap onto it.

Photo by James Crisp

It works great!

I've tried many capos and I finally settled on a brand that doesn't pull the strings when you set the capo on a fret. I was using the Shubb capo for a long time, but every time I clamped it down on a new fret, it would slightly pull the strings off tune a bit. This is because the angle of the Shubb clamp is off center to the neck, literally pulling the strings to the side a bit. I know a lot of players who clamp these suckers down tighter than a gnat's ass on an ice cube. Too much pressure on a capo will absolutely cause tuning problems, folks! The best one I've found is a Paige banjo capo. It clamps up from the bottom center, not off center like the Schubb, therefore guaranteeing equal pressure on all strings. Hey, J.D. Crowe uses it, and that's good enough for me... (Let me mention, though, I found the Shubb capo to work best on my Martin D-35s and D-28s, and I use Shubb exclusively on my guitars).

My Vega PS-5 long neck is a rare classic. They are not made anymore and hard to find. As I mentioned earlier in this book, I found mine from a classified ad in the back of a three-year-old issue of FRETS Magazine, two years after they ceased publication. When the instrument arrived via UPS a few days later, I opened the package to find this beautiful banjo in perfect condition. So, I know they are still out there. As I said, the Vega PS-5 is patterned exactly after the model that Pete Seeger invented, and I absolutely LOVE it's unique sound.

Keep your eye on classified sections of magazines like 5-*String Quarterly*. Pass the word around music festivals that you're looking for one. Contact your local luthier. Instrument makers like Homer Ledford in Winchester, Kentucky are great resources in locating old instruments. Homer found me an extra Vega long neck "NECK" for only $50!

However, some companies continue to make a pretty fair sounding long neck. The Deering Company comes to mind. They have two models that are actually excellent, and fairly affordable. They are worth the purchase price, for sure. When compared to the old Vega, the Deering banjo is a bit more brittle sounding, but you might prefer that kind of sound to the warmer, more muted tones of the Vega.

I encourage you to at least try this unique instrument. Its versatility and sound are unmatched. It stands out in a crowded field of Gibson Mastertones, at the very least. By simply putting a capo on the third fret, you have a banjo you can play in all the standard tunings and positions.

But those extra three frets...man, those three frets offer a whole new musical world for this instrument that needs to be explored by players much better than myself.

If you have any thoughts, experiences, or songs, go ahead and get in touch with me. I'd love to hear your ideas.

Cosmic Banjo

Instrumental by Michael Johnathon

Music Tableture by John Roberts

You might want to listen to the CD first before you attempt this. This song was recorded with a rock band, a French horn quartet and my long-neck banjo, tuned all the way down the neck.   LONG-NECK BANJO

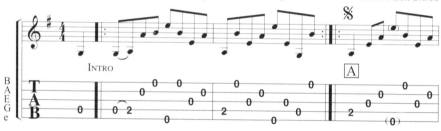

Last time to Coda ⊕

Kentucky Korn Puddin'

the real thing

I shall fall in love with and marry any woman who can make this.
I shall salute and honor any man who can cook this.
I shall uphold and fight for any law that protects this.
I shall serve and protect any nation that demands this.
I shall frequent any restaurant that will add this to the menu.
I shall travel any distance, climb any mountain, swim any ocean, walk any mile in any man's shoes...I will even watch MTV if I have to, in order to receive all the passion and poetry offered by the savory succulence of this copious corn concoction.

Oh, I luv corn puddin'!

4 eggs
1/4 cup of sugar
1 teaspoon of salt
2 pints of whole or 2% milk
8 tablespoons of general purpose flour
2 cups whole kernel corn (fresh or frozen, not canned)
4 rounded teaspoons of real butter
(not margarine...using margarine instead of butter is like dating a blow-up doll instead of a real woman)

STEP ONE: melt the butter

STEP TWO: in a large bowl, pour in the melted butter, then
              add the corn, flour, salt and sugar.

STEP THREE: In a smaller bowl, beat up the eggs, mix in the milk and
              add into the corn mixture.

STEP FOUR: Pour mixture into a medium sized, lightly greased, baking pan.

Bake slowly in the oven at a 300 degree heat for about 40 to 45 minutes. Stir the pan from the bottom about every 15 minutes while it's baking.

Served best with your relatives over for dinner.

For the corn to bake properly, you must play Bill Monroe, the McLain Family Band, Hylo Brown, Jean Ritchie or any other Korn-tucky music while cooking.

"the 𝕭-word"

bitch (b≤ch) *n:*
1. A female animal, especially a dog.
2. *Offensive.* A woman considered spiteful or overbearing.
3. *Slang.* A complaint from a female.
4. *Slang.* Something very unpleasant or difficult.

AMERICAN HERITAGE DICTIONARY

I'm not trying to justify its use.
I'm not making fun of anybody.
And I'm *not* trying to be rude toward women.
However, it's the absolute truth and an undeniable fact...it's also kind of funny when you think about it:

There is no one-syllable word in the English language that women can use when referring to men that has the equal social and personal impact men have when using the word *"Bitch"*.

No phrase has ever been created for females to deploy that can produce the same, all-encompassing, knee-jerk, emotional hot-fire reaction that a man can ignite when referring to a woman as a *"Bitch"*.

No term exists in any language that is so completely gender specific and reduces the very essence of a human being down to the barest, most basic cliche' as does the term *"Bitch"*.

Go ahead, try to find one...I *dare* you.

127

First of all, most names women have for men are *two-syllable*, which instantly disqualifies the moniker.

Second, most of the other words are *not* gender specific. You can call a man an "idiot", for example, but you CAN'T refer to him as a "bitch". Unless, of course, well...we won't get into that here.

Third, the balance of her available words have their impact neutralized because the terms are sexual in definition. You see, women fail to realize that the majority of men appreciate all references to sex, even when they are negative towards his person. It just doesn't matter. The male nature is to be grateful for any attention he can muster in that department.

For example, a woman might get justifiably angry towards a fellow, and call him a "bastard". The problem she faces here is twofold:

a) the term "bastard" has more than one syllable, which automatically disqualifies it for consideration.
b) the very meaning of the word heavily implies that, once upon a time, *somebody* had sex.

Hey, no man will get angry over that!

As I pointed out, most men applaud any event, catalyst, or verbal trigger that will get their woman to refer to sex, even if the term is laced in various stages of personal disdain. So long as the term has a sexual overtone of *some kind*, the man wins and the woman automatically looses the verbal battle.

But...

...call a woman a "Bitch" and you will unleash a genetic firestorm that swells from the bottom of her bunched up panties to the top of her flaming eyeballs. Proving thusly, to all observers, that she might very well be exactly as so described.

Nope, women are at a linguistic loss here...no word is within their reach that will come close to the power of that one-syllable marvel.

Just make sure you duck
if you use it...

CPeaA Summer Salad

a recipe

I finally understand the fundamental difference between the sexes: Girls like Bob Villa...and guys like Norm.

It explains everything. If you've ever watched the "New Yankee Workshop" on PBS, you know what I mean . . .

. . . just felt like pointing that out.

This recipe offers a wonderful, cool and lo-calorie taste of summer you can have all year long. I got this from a good friend of mine, Tammy Farley, from Lexington, Kentucky. She and her husband, Mark, are big music fans and have been very supportive of my various music projects during the past several years. Mark also happens to be quite a craftsman, sort of Kentucky's own version of Norm.

As for Tammy, she's a Certified Public Accountant by trade who also happens to be a great cook. Of course, I'm not implying here that she cooks anything but food. She's so honest that she first verifies the number of peas used in the recipe, writes a receipt and then makes you sign it before she commences making this concoction.

Just layer the following in a big salad bowl (keep the stuff in order!)

1/2 head of lettuce torn into bite-size pieces
1/4 cup shredded cheddar cheese
1/4 cup chopped green bell peppers
1/2 package of sweet peas
   (par-boil these suckers 'bout 5 minutes first)

1/4 cup of sweet onions
1/4 cup chopped celery
1/4 cup bacon bits

Spread 1/2 pint of Miracle Whip over the top of the salad, "sealing" the edges against the bowl. Sprinkle 1/2 tablespoon of white sugar on top.

Then set it in the 'fridge about 6 hours.

That's right...6 hours.

When you're ready to serve this addictive entreé to your guests, get a big wooden spoon and first mix it all up.

First time I experienced my "pea salad high", I was hooked for life. If I could dispense this in a syringe and mainline it, I would. Served best with iced tea for lunch while building a dual compartment, six-drawer, colonial style dining room hutch with cherry wood trim. Music? A Malcolm Dalgish hammer dulcimer CD, of course.

Serves a half-dozen normal people, or one pea-lovin' folksinger like me.

Summer Honeymoon

Words and Music by
Michael Johnathon
©1995 Rachel-Aubrey Music/BMI
as performed on the CD "WoodSongs"

Play this happy, like you're standing
around a gazebo in the middle of a park
on a sunny Sunday afternoon.

Summer Honeymoon

Well, I know - that you want - to have a man by your side
Well, I'll be yours someday
But a girl in Love don't have no mind to wait
So I'll be yours right away

"Get it on, get it up, get it over with," you say
I'll be yours someday
But you think if you wait you're gonna run out of time to play
So I'll be yours right away

So, Hold on
Wait a minute
I'm catchin' up real soon
I'll be your baby on a
Summer Honeymoon

Just give me time to remember
What tomorrow used to be
And I'll be yours right away...

whole verse instrumental

So, Hold on
Wait a minute
I'm catchin' up real soon
I'll be your baby on a
Summer Honeymoon

So hurry up, pack it in, I'm getting older every day
I'll be yours someday
Tomorrow is a gift
Left over from today
So I'll be yours right away

I'll be your...
I'll be your little baby...
Right away!

Heroes

*"Show me a hero,
and I'll show you a tragedy..."*
F. Scott Fitzgerald

It's time we become our *own* heroes.
That, I believe, is how heroes are made.
And another thing...a real hero doesn't need a publicist.

The hero making Industry is a huge, billion-dollar corporate Goliath. Most of us, the customers, become the victims of this "factory". We, the adoring public, make for a grand, easily sold, fertile marketplace.
Why?
Because we all so desperately want to believe that someone, somewhere is bigger, better and bolder than we are. We reject our own imperfections by infusing perfection into someone else. We are so disappointed in ourselves that we look to other imperfect humans for signs of the physical and moral qualities we so desperately lack.
The Industry that creates these heroes for us is very smart and shrewd. They surround us with constant reminders of our imperfections and tendencies for failure.
How?
By inundating our eyes, ears and spirit with images of what *they* consider to be a "perfect" person. We see them everywhere. On billboards, TV commercials, magazines, music videos and CD covers. Photos of slender models with computer corrected skin and artificially perky breasts *(well, maybe that part ain't so bad...)* who look nothing like any woman I've ever seen, rendering "normal" women as unsatisfactory. Chiseled men with heads of thick, surgically implanted hair who are paid a full-time wage to develop washboard bellies and make looking at ourselves in mirrors painful post-shower episodes.
Why?
To sell *stuff*, of course.
The creations of this Industry, the Heroes, are usually unhappy, empty-hearted people who simply have the ability to afford the price needed to publicize the manufactured image that was created in their behalf. Created, usually, by marketing people. The marketing people use the Heroes to sell you the stuff made by the corporations who employ them. If the Hero is, say, a basketball player, then the product is a game ticket and a line of sneakers, or some other endorsement. It should come as no surprise that every

team in every town actively publicizes its own Heroes.

How long?

Only for as long as our Hero has the ability to sell the company's stuff.

And not a second longer.

Babe Ruth was a hero that did heroic things in the sports world. When Babe Ruth could no longer sell tickets to the public, his Hero status was promptly removed and he was unceremoniously dismissed from the Yankees. Today, it seems that every sports team has the biggest, baddest, bestest *whatever* of all time.

But, unlike Babe Ruth, they are unable to transcend their own hype. Years after the hoopla and the marketing and the publicity was over, lo and behold, people realized that ol' Babe Ruth actually *did* stuff. He accomplished something that warranted admiration.

Babe Ruth, with regards his sports accomplishments, actually was a hero. But even so, like I pointed out before, time has also revealed how shallow and sad his life was. He was an empty shell wearing Heroes clothing.

So, I don't care if it's a leader of a nation, an actor in a movie or, like those in my profession, a musician or singer...modern day Heroes are mostly Lies and we are royally *stupid* if we let ourselves go along with it. Actually, I think the people in my business are the worst of the bunch.

Let me explain.

Musicians, you see, do nothing greater than vibrate air for a living.

That's it.

Period.

Music is simply air molecules hitting and shaking and colliding around a room. Musicians are lucky people who get to vibrate air with a certain sense of order against your eardrums for a living. You either like the bouncing air or not.

"What is so Heroic about that?" I ask.

"Not a thing," I answer back.

Yet we have created virtual Gods out of these shallow-minded, vain, overpaid air-shakers in an effort to sell CDs and tapes and concert tickets. And that's the beginning and the end of it.

These godlike, musical Nephelim walk the earth until the day that we, the public, come to our senses and notice, *"Hey! They've got gray hair like me! Their marriage is as bad as mine! She's getting fat around the hips like my wife!"*

Or, worst of all: *"Dear God, They're getting...old."*

The most over inflated of these godlike ones, Michael Jackson, recently crashed to earth with a deafening, tremendous roar. His fall from greatness was measured, not in the moral analysis of his achievements or lack thereof, but in the decline of his worldwide product sales.

Greatness was once measured by the power of our spirit

overcoming all odds. Now, it's measured by SoundScan and bar codes.

Have we, as a human family, learned anything from this? Do we protect ourselves and our children from spiritual and moral disappointment by shunning this human Hero assembly line?

Heck, no.

It just keeps getting worse.

Just look at the fashion industry.

Young impressionable girls *(who don't know a thing about what men want)* yearn and ache to be just like their emaciated supermodel heroes *(who don't know a thing about what men want)* who in turn are dressed by gay fashion designers *(who don't know a thing about what straight men want)* whose goals are to sell clothes to the impressionable young girls...

... in order for them to be attractive to men. What?

Who thought up this crap, anyway?

Let's face it, fashion models are the goofiest of all manufactured heroes. I'm not coming down on models or the general idea of it. Hey, if it's what you want, go for it. But let's be honest here-

Supermodels are an American disaster.

They cause damage simply by existing.

Why?

Because, in order for the fashion industry to create "heroes" (those fashion super-models from Twiggy to Kate Moss who will stand apart from the public and sell their products) they have to get you to hate your body.

They sell their stuff by getting you to hate your body?

Damn right.

And it works, too.

Did you know that in the USA 40% of young girls have a negative body image? That 50% of American girls ages nine to sixteen years old are on diets? Why would a twelve year old girl give a rat's ass about what a man wants? SHE DOESN'T! She's emulating the supermodel, that's all. I don't know who's dumber, the over-paid model whose only talent is dieting and "walking", or the parents who allow their daughters to be taken in by this crap.

Young American women are starving themselves, taking drugs, becoming anorexic and generally making themselves miserable so they can emulate their skeletal, emaciated fashion Goddesses, who are *also* miserable (mainly because they can't eat). By the time they reach adulthood, one out of three of these girls not only end up overweight with horribly low self esteem but spent *thousands of dollars* on stuff the fashion models sold them.

And what about these so-called supermodels...the "heroes" used by gay fashion designers to sell clothes to women who want to be attractive to straight men? The minute they begin looking the least bit human, they are tossed off the runway. The instant they start looking like...*the customers,* they're finished.

It happens over and over and you'd think we'd know better by now...but we don't. It's like a self-imposed treadmill.

We're busy creating and searching for replacement idols every day. Should one Hero fall off the assembly line, the Hero Industry simply looks for new Heroes to replace those who have dared to expose their humanity.

And, like cattle or idiots, or both, we go along with it.

So, my question is this:

What is so wrong with looking for these heroic qualities inside of our own selves? Why can't we infuse these things in our children instead of baseball players, actors and supermodels? Why can't we learn to lead *ourselves* instead of asking entertainers or politicians and governments to do it for us?

I'm not talking about surrendering our sense of order. To the contrary. Governments and leaders, in their place, serve a valuable purpose. So do models, for that matter. After all, I want to see what a shirt or jacket looks like before I buy it.

I'm talking about surrendering our sense of *inner* leadership, *inner* example, and *inner* contentment.

The best defense against corporate Heroes is simply to become our own Hero. Be what we want others to be. Accomplish good and honorable deeds of our *own.* We need to develop the sense of honesty, morality, integrity and love that we want our "heroes" to have. If we have these things inside our own selves, we won't need these cookie-cutter media hyped imitators.

Think of the benefits...

Our confidence and independence will transcend corporate marketing. We will start making decisions based on our own judgment instead of media and advertising pressure.

We will seek out and explore music that we *like,* not just because it is number one on the hit parade. We will appreciate actors because of their skills, not because "he's so cute" or "she's got a great body." We will start to define our individual roles in our communities again, something we stopped doing a generation ago.

The best thing, I think, will come from the results born of our carrying these heroic mantles on our own shoulders. Heroic actions will become real, not created and marketed for commercial purposes. Our self esteem will rise as we shed the conviction that others are more worthy than we are, that others are better than we are, or that others deserve more than we do. In balance, I believe we can all be Heroes of some kind.

My advice, for what little it is worth, is this:

Be a hero in *your* world, not *the* world.

"What the heck does that mean?" you ask.

This...

Simply define the outer reaches of your influence, and then do the best you can to achieve the most good within those borders.

And it's not nearly as complicated as I made that sound. Let me explain what I mean about *"defining the outer reaches of your influence"*:

If you are the President of the United States, your influence for good reaches around the globe and across every state in this nation. If you are the Mayor of a town, your field of influence goes across every neighborhood within that city. If you are a teacher, it is the heart and mind of every student in your classroom. If you are a laborer on an assembly line, it is the community of your co-workers.

On the other hand, if you are a musician, your influence goes past the limits of your imagination and outward, well beyond the furthermost reaches of the most distant radio signal that will play your music. Your world of influence can go up to a satellite and around the planet in an instant. What a magnificent opportunity that is, unfortunately, used mostly for selling stuff...*sigh.*

The trick, however, is to be sure NOT to reach beyond your sphere of influence. It will lead to frustration and you will quit before accomplishing a darn thing.

Here's an example:

Let's say you are a Mom. Your world of influence is your family. Does the homeless problem bother you and you are moved to help? Good!

DON'T try to *cure* the problem.

You can't.

Your influence doesn't reach that far.

So, what can a Mom do? Bake an extra loaf of bread and bring it to the local homeless shelter each week is one idea that comes to mind. Maybe you can think of another. I can guarantee you that a hungry 10 year old child doesn't give a rat's pitutee who's #1 on the pop charts when they are diving into morsels of fresh, hot buttered sourdough bread while living in a shelter. You will be a Hero to that child. If you are a working man, then buy an extra blanket or coat or shirt and donate it to the shelter. By helping the homeless and the agencies that help them, you are helping to cure the homeless problem.

By enhancing the world around you, you become a Hero to that world. Michael Jackson or Pete Rose or OJ Simpson have contributed NOTHING to the world at large that will exceed the value of a dad telling his children he loves them. Or of a wife kissing her husband with true passion. NOTHING!

All they ever did was sell stuff.

Big deal.

There is an old saying that originated, I believe, from the Ukraine or Germany. The saying was, simply,

"If everyone in the whole world
simply took care of their own homes,
you wouldn't have to worry about the world anymore."

Isn't that beautiful? In the 1960's some very astute biologist named Rene´ Dubos broke the lesson all the way down to bumper sticker size with:

"Think globally, act locally".

So, what does it all mean?

This:

If you claim, for example, to be concerned about the environment, then get out there and clean up your *own* yard. If your yard is clean, organize your family to go clean up a nearby creek or highway or park. Shucks, if everyone in the whole world simply cleaned up their own yards, think of the changes it would bring! Think of how clean our neighborhoods and cities and country would be. Think of the respect for our land that our kids would learn and, in turn, pass on to *their* kids.

And who's the Hero that accomplished this?

You!

And another thing, contribute to the solution of problems you are concerned about with a smile. That, my friends, is a Hero. If you are a musician, use your music in ways that will transcend money and fame. When you have a chance to sing and speak about the environment, war or civil rights, JUST DO IT.

You *don't* have to talk about your new album all the time.

On the other hand, when not talking about their new albums, artists like Oasis, Michael Jackson, Madonna and Alan Jackson talk about... uuh... hmmm... let's see...I'm at a loss here...

Again, it's just my opinion, but one of the biggest problems with the entertainment business is that darned spotlight. It's like a shot of heroin to the recipient and it's a voyeuristic liar. It places tremendous power and privilege into the hands of three chord idiots. I think the human mind is an awesome, magnificent creative force. To have a thousand or more of these miraculous minds focused on your words and music for an entire concert performance is an unbelievable privilege and responsibility. To bring joy and music and emotion to them is a brilliant use of the art form.

And it's a mighty fine rush, too.

Yet, as a musician, all we can possibly do is vibrate air.

The spotlight, however, amplifies that minor achievement beyond reason. The spotlight somehow implies greatness in a world of mediocrity, and it is so easily believed by most of us.

A singer and his songs will never accomplish anything greater or more critical to your life than, say, a plumber who fixes your bathroom on a holiday weekend...

...but no one ever gave that plumber a standing ovation for a job well done.

"In hell, people have chopsticks a yard long
and cannot feed themselves.
In heaven, the chopsticks are also a yard long,
but the people feed each other..."
Vietnamese wisdom

The Internet

Like the human mind, the internet will prove to be an untapped pool of brilliant banality. Here we are, connected to the whole world with a single stroke on a keyboard, but we seem to lack anything important to say. We have no great knowledge to accept, no grand wisdom to impart. All we do with this magnificent technology is attempt to sell *stuff*.

That makes the internet nothing more than an upscale street market that refuses to accept cash.

by the way, my home page is:
http://members.aol.com/PoetUSA/home.html

The Hero and the Maiden

a story

Once upon a time,

there was a beautiful young maiden.
    And for a while,
        she loved a young man with all her heart.
And forever the young man thought he would wear her love like a
crown upon his soul.

    One day, dark clouds came spilling over the mountaintops,
and the rain fell. The maiden became frightened and disappointed
because the young man was unable to make the rain stop and the
thunder cease.
    So, she became bitter towards him and said,
"I do not love you anymore. You are not the one for me."

And the young man stood alone in the rain,
    his heart broken in two
        as he watched the young maiden run away,
          forever.

    Soon, the dark clouds began to thin, the thunder ceased,
and the sun dried the wet ground and warmed the young man's
    shoulders.
    After a while, the young man realized that although
he missed being loved and the feeling of being in love...
    ...he didn't miss the foolish young maiden after all.
        He is a Hero.

Alice Lloyd and Abisha Johnson about 1925

Photo courtesy of Alice Lloyd College archives

Miracle On Caney Creek

"Life begets life...Energy begets energy.
It is by spending oneself that one becomes rich."
Sarah Bernhardt

ALICE LLOYD COLLEGE
Renowned mountain school located eight miles east. Alice Lloyd came from Boston, 1916, dedicating her life to education of youth in area. Caney Creek Community Center was organized, 1917, Caney Junior College, 1923. After her death, 1962, college renamed honoring founder, who inspired graduates to serve this region. Supported by friends throughout U.S.

Let me tell you the true story about a real hero...

While I was in Mousie roaming the mountain hollers each day, I always kept an ear out for unusual or moving stories. One afternoon while visiting a friend in Hindman, I happened upon a book written by a Dr. Jerry Davis which I found to be particularly enchanting. By sunset, I not only had finished the book, but also began writing a song called *Miracle On Caney Creek*.

It's about Alice Lloyd, an extraordinary woman who settled into the Appalachian mountains and lived an astounding life.

I'd like to share her story with you.

We begin in Boston in the autumn of 1916.

Alice is a 40 year old journalist who finds herself hospitalized after suffering a stroke and then contracting spinal meningitis. Her doctor gives her six months to live. However, he adds, she could possibly extend her life another two years if she moves south to a warmer climate and away from the bitter cold of the Boston harbor.

Her husband, Arthur, looks upon his crippled wife with disdain. She has lost most of her ability to control her left side and can only hobble around now, using her right hand to aid herself.

Upon hearing the doctor's advice, her husband bristles and tells Alice, *"One life wasted is unavoidable, two lives wasted is senseless."* Arthur, who preceded O.J. in the wife abuse department by over a half century, then abandons Alice to her illness and ultimate demise.

Meanwhile, Alice's pastor in her Boston church learns of her plight and of the doctor's instructions. He comes to her aid with a possible solution. It seems the church owns some property in a little hamlet in Knott County, Kentucky. The church had once used it as a missionary home, but it was now abandoned. Alice was welcome to have full use of the little cabin and property for as long as it was needed. Kentucky was certainly warmer than Boston, plus she could have it for free.

But the generous offer also came with a warning:

The church's missionaries were not well received, it seems, as the local men had run them off with shotguns. The mountain folks obviously did not take well to outsiders.

Distressed by Arthur's unsupportive actions, her illness and the time limit on her life, she accepts the church's offer in spite of the pastor's warning.

Alice Lloyd arrives in the mountain community of Hindman, Kentucky in November of 1916. She is accompanied only by her aging mother, Mrs. Geddes.

They find the little, windowless church cabin abandoned and in disrepair. They fix it up as best they can and settle in for a long winter.

In February, 1917, just a few months later, a very odd thing happens.

A mountain man named Abisha Johnson, who lives in the same county just a few miles away, hears about the two *"firren wimin"* who had recently moved into the area. These two women, he was told, were educated ladies from *"Amerikay"*, the land beyond the mountains.

Now, Abisha is a sincere, humble mountain man. A hard worker with a large family. He is 55 years old and very ill. He's humpbacked yet still manages to support his wife and their 11 children on his small piece of land.

On this cold February night, Abisha has a fitful sleep. He dreams that the *"firren womin"* will teach his children to read the Bible, making them, in his words, *"...unliken the hogs"*.

You see, Abisha has a harsh view of life in Appalachia.

Caney Holler in Knott County, Kentucky about 1920.

He sees his family trapped, confined to the hills like farm hogs in a barnyard. He wanted to break free, but couldn't. He felt you were born, you bred and then you died just like animals...all the while ensnared by the poverty of the "barnyard", or, in his mind, the mountains.

He desperately wanted a way out of that cycle for his children. He felt if only this stranger woman could teach his children to read, they would be educated and able to lift themselves up from his poverty.

Well, Abisha awakens from his dream and, barefoot (yes, barefoot), crosses two mountains in a snowstorm until he finds Alice's cabin. Freezing and weak, he collapses through her door and begs her to come help his children.

He offers her an unusual proposition on this cold winter night.

He wants Alice and Mrs. Geddes to move across the county to his mountain holler along the Caney Creek. He begs her to come help his children and the children of his friends, and teach them to read the Bible. He even promises to build a better cabin for Alice to live in... with windows, if she wants.

And, if she will do this, he vows to give Alice his land.
His land...

In the world of mountain life, Abisha offered Alice the most valuable, most precious thing he had. Land was life itself, and he offered it *all* to Alice. That's how much Abisha loved his children.

Alice accepts his offer, and in the spring of 1917, she and her mother move onto Abisha's property on Caney Creek and begin a small community school. *(Today, Abisha Johnson's land is the campus property of what has come to be known as Alice Lloyd College).*

What happens to them over the course of the next several decades is truly amazing.

Alice and her mother start the little school, as she promised. The reaction by the mountain folks is immediate and most certainly positive.

Too positive, actually.

Dozens of families send their children to Alice and Mrs. Geddes for *"the larnin' at the Caney School"*.

However, an immediate problem they face is the fact that the local children are from very poor families. There is no money to buy the supplies they need to build classrooms, to obtain books and paper, or purchase teaching equipment, like chalkboards.

Their limited resources become strained to the breaking point, almost from day one.

So, Alice makes an agreement with the local men.

She will somehow find the money needed to construct the school and teach the children *tuition free* ...if they promise to provide the labor she needs to build the classrooms and care for the school property.

The mountain men agree, but on yet one more condition: *Alice must also promise not to meddle in their religion, their politics, or their moonshining.*

With that simple understanding, she embarks upon a quest that spans the next several decades as she searchs to find the money needed to keep the school going. She begins by writing letters to friends, colleagues and wealthy people across the country, asking for help. She writes dozens of letters each day. The only means Alice has to accomplish this is an old, cumbersome Oliver #9 typewriter.

If you are ever able to visit Alice Lloyd College in Pippa Passes, Kentucky, you will be able to go into Alice's small cabin office where she spent most of her life. In that office there is a large file cabinet which contains the documented records of *over 60,000 letters* Alice herself wrote to people all over America, searching for gifts of money, books, paper, supplies, volunteer help... anything to help support the school on Caney Creek.

For years, Alice Lloyd could be seen hunched over her desk, laboring away from dawn till dusk, pecking away on her typewriter writing letters.

One of the letters finds its way onto the information board in a woman's dormitory at Wesleyan College, located in upstate New York. Among the readers is a student, Miss June Buchanan. She is moved by the idea of teaching kids in Appalachia and volunteers to help during the summer of 1919 *(June stayed until her death in 1989. She was 99 years old).*

Miss June brings a wealth of art and energy to Caney. Her generous personality helps compliment the more reserved, business-like tone of Alice Lloyd. One of Miss June's major contributions to the school is the writings of Robert Browning. His poem *Pippa's Song* becomes a staple of the students educational menu through the years. It is from this poem that Alice eventually finds a name for the college post office (thus the name *Pippa Pass,* later changed to *Pippa Passes*).

During the next several years, the school and the local community grow and flourish together. But not without some dramatic moments. There are a few people in the region who deeply resent Alice's "outsider" presence and show it, often violently. She is shot at, harassed and spurned on many occasions. Someone even burned a dormitory building down. But through it all, the community at large rallies to her aid, and the school presses on. Alice never gives up, nor does she forget her promise to Abisha Johnson. She tells the students after each crisis *"...You must have aspirations as high as the mountains, and faith as firm as the rocks".*

The school makes its way into the early 1950's. America has just survived a turbulant global war, atomic bomb explosions, a massive depression and drastic social upheaval. Now the war is over, and the nation breathes a huge sigh of relief as it gets on with the business of making America materially rich again.

The mountain communities, however, find no relief in this

new found national confidence. The war years were hard enough, but during peacetime demand for coal that fueled the great war machine becomes virtually nonexistent. As the rest of the nation goes back to work, the coal mining region of the mountains plunges into its deepest, darkest economic quandary of all time.

The financial fortunes of Alice's school rise and fall along with those of the mountain community. By 1953, Alice is no longer able to pay teachers' salaries or workmen's wages at the school.

Simply put, Alice runs out of money.

Most are willing to stay on, but the future looks bleak. Volunteer attorneys for the school recommend drastic action.

Alice must file for bankruptcy, soon.

The Caney School? Bankrupt? After everything they've been through and struggled for? After all these years of scraping by and surviving?

There is no choice.

That spring, at the Knott County courthouse in Hindman, papers are drawn up that will eventually bankrupt Alice's school and end her promise to Abisha, made in faith so many years before.

However...

About this same time, a very wealthy man dies in New Jersey.

Years ago, the man had received a letter from a certain Alice Lloyd from a place called Pippa Pass, Kentucky. It was a simple, direct and bold letter that moved him to financially help out the school.

So, every year since then, Lamont DuPont, chairman of the mighty DuPont Chemical Corporation, would send in his personal gift to Alice Lloyd at Christmas time.

After his death, Mr. DuPont's personal accountant began the task of closing his personal affairs and kept coming across a yearly entry of money sent to some unknown woman in a small, obscure Kentucky town.

Well, well, well...

...it was "obvious" to Mr. Accountant that ol' Lamont left behind a bit of a surprise for his widowed wife and family. Not wanting to give this unaccounted for "heir" a chance to cause damage by making future claims against the DuPont fortune, DuPont's widow sends the accountant to Kentucky with a suitcase full of cash to "...pay the little hussy off".

Days later, the accountant makes his way by car into the mountains. He travels along the cramped, curving roads past coal mines, lumbered mountains and small cabins. He steers his motor car along a small creek as he nears Pippa Pass. Soon, the road bends around a sharp curve and the cramped, narrow holler suddenly expands before his eyes.

There before him is his destination...a school, 600 students and a crippled little old lady named Alice Lloyd!

No words can describe the surprise of this little bean counter.

Alice Lloyd about 1925

He discovers that the yearly entry in his late employer's ledger was nothing more than Mr. DuPont's response to a letter Alice sent him nearly twenty years ago. So, he sheepishly leaves behind the suitcase of cash as a final contribution to the school and returns to the equally surprised, and relieved, DuPont family in New Jersey.

      The accountant can't get his experience out of his mind and he tells the story to many of his friends. Among them, a writer named William Bennett. Bennett, in turn, takes the story and writes an article. He sends the manuscript to his close buddy who happens to be the editor of a national magazine.

A few weeks later, a story entitled *"Stay On Stranger"* appears in Readers Digest Magazine.

Alas, neither a suitcase full of cash nor a national magazine article is enough to cure the financial damage done to the school, and bankruptcy proceedings continue at the local courthouse.

Meanwhile, across the country on the west coast, a pretty blonde secretary carries in the day's mail and places it on her boss' desk. In between meetings and phone calls, the man sorts his way down the pile and comes upon the new issue of his favorite magazine, Readers Digest. While half-listening to the conversations of other executives in his Hollywood office, he reads the incredible story of Alice Lloyd and her little school in the mountains of Kentucky.

The man is Ralph Edwards, executive producer and host of the popular TV show *"This Is Your Life"* on the NBC television network.

His decision is swift and immediate.

He wants that woman on his show...*Now!*

Researchers and co-producers scrambl to locate this woman from the isolated Appalachian mountains of America. They finally contact an attorney in Hindman, Dan Martin, for help. Dan also happens to be a former Caney student.

They call him on the phone.

Yes, he knows Alice. Yes, he could ask her. Certainly, he'll phone back as soon as she decides.

Dan Martin explains the situation to June Buchanan and Commador Slone, two of Alice's most trusted friends. They know getting Alice to Hollywood, California will be no easy task. Not only is she old and very ill, *but she hasn't left Caney holler in 26 years!*

But try they must. Putting Alice on national television is probably the last chance they have to save the school.

So, they go to Alice...and lie.

They tell her a very wealthy man wants to donate a large gift to the Caney School, but he's too busy to come to Kentucky. She must go to the benefactor and thank him for the gift.

To save her school, Alice loads her crippled, frail body into a car and heads to the nearest train depot, two hours away. She then painfully boards a train in Hazard, Kentucky for the three day ride to Hollywood, California.

Soon enough, the moment of the TV broadcast arrives.

Alice, unaware of what is happening, sits on a couch in what seems to be a rather odd looking living room. The large curtain in front of her suddenly parts to the glare of bright lights and the sound of applause. The voice of an unseen announcer tells her through the large studio speakers,

"Alice Lloyd of Pippa Pass, Kentucky...This Is Your Life!"
For the next 30 minutes, Alice listens to the account of her life

as told by friends and former students. People like John Hall, chairman of Armco Steel, Carl D. Perkins, one of the most powerful congressmen in Washington, DC, June Buchanan, Commador Slone and others. The story of her school, her dreams and her promise to Abisha Johnson is disclosed in full on network television.

Ralph Edwards is so moved by the courage of this frail woman that, at the end of the broadcast, he turns to the camera and spontaneously addresses his national audience face to face and says:

"Please, let's all send a dollar, or five dollars or whatever you can afford. Let's all help Miss Lloyd's dream stay alive".

Alice Lloyd and Ralph Edwards during her appearance on NBC-TV's prime time show "This Is Your Life".

As he speaks, Alice's address is flashed on the TV screen.

Two days later, as Alice and company are en route back to Kentucky, the sheriff in Hazard gets a frantic phone call from the postmaster in Lexington. Slamming the phone down, the sheriff rushes into the street and grabs the first fourteen men he finds. He deputizes them, arms them with shotguns and has them surround the Hazard post office to wait for a large shipment of mail coming in from Lexington.

About late afternoon, several trucks lumber into Hazard carrying bags of mail addressed to Alice Lloyd.

Today, hanging on the office wall of Mr. C. Vernon Cooper, the president of Peoples Bank in Hazard, is the photo of a table piled high with *268,000 dollar bills...* money mailed in to Alice Lloyd by caring people from around the nation, people who wanted to help keep her dream alive.

Here's a "little" of the flood money that started pouring into Caney Community Center after its founder, Mrs. Alice Lloyd, appeared ont he TV show "This Is Your Life." Male students of Caney Junior College sort the letters in the print shop. Carefull records of all these gifts are being kept. (Louisville Courier-Journal photo by Thomas V. Miller, Jr.)

The afternoon that I read Dr. Jerry Davis' book about Alice, I recall walking to a nearby swinging bridge stretched across two hollers. I sat on the bridge with my guitar and just envisioned this spectacular, true story that I just read about. I began to write a melody that reminded me of the feeling I had while reading the book.

But the words didn't come.

The next day, I looked up "Alice Lloyd College" in the Knott County phone book and called. The receptionist answered and I asked for Alice Lloyd.

"Well," she explained, "Alice Lloyd passed on years ago."

Ok, I'm a jerk.

So, I hesitantly asked about June Buchanan.

"Yes, Miss June is here," she says, and I was put on hold. Miss June finally answered and I told her what I was doing.

"Well, well," she replies, "Why don't you just stop by for a visit, then?"

That afternoon, I headed to the beautiful mountain campus of Alice Lloyd College. Among the mix of new buildings and rustic cabins was the small fieldstone home of June Buchanan. We sat on her front porch, sipping hot tea and nibbling blackberry muffins as she told me the story of her life on Caney.

Dr. Jerry Davis, it turns out, was also the president of Alice Lloyd College. He eventually joined us, too.

I was so taken with the story and the events of the day that I walked over to the campus coffee shop after my visit with June and wrote the lyrics to *Miracle On Caney Creek* on the back of a napkin.

About two years later, after *The Passing* concert tour was over, I decided it was time to bring the song and Alice's story to life.

So, I approached Pepsi USA and John DuPuy III, the Pikeville Pepsi distributor, with an idea:

I wanted them to finance a project to make a music video of the song *Miracle On Caney Creek*, even though their company logo would not be shown or bottles of pop would not be seen in the clip.

They said "Yes."

It didn't seem to matter that I had never in my life filmed a music video before.

Well, we not only made the five minute music video on 35mm film but, with the help of many actors and volunteers *(folks like Phyllis Reynolds, Elizebeth Spicer, Kevin Mann, Sid Johnson and others)* from the University of Kentucky and the University of Louisville, we also taped a 25 minute docu-drama *(an acted-out documentary)* on Alice and June's life on video. Ralph Edwards, who remains on the Alice Lloyd College board of directors even today, donated the actual footage of Alice Lloyd and Miss June appearing on his TV show for use in the docu-drama.

We put the 25 minute docu-drama and 5 minute video together on one 30 minute VHS tape, printed a nice jacket and had it distributed free of charge to nearly 2,000 schools and libraries in Appalachia. Teachers from Jessamine County middle school wrote a class curriculum that went with it. The music video was shown on TNN, PBS, VH-1 and went on to become the number 12 video on Country Music Television (with no record release!).

Cast and crew members of the "Miracle On Caney Creek" music video.

In 1916, Alice Lloyd was told she had six months to live.

She could have shriveled up inside herself and drowned in her own self pity, but she didn't. Alice found a purpose for the time she thought she had left, and invested every moment with great passion and success. Over 3,000 of her students became teachers in the 118 mountain schools that she helped start. Her students became doctors, lawyers, poets and professionals. They became powerful congressmen, gubernatorial candidates, heads of major corporations, and administrators.

They all received a *tuition free education,* from grammar school through college. If they did well, she even paid their way to better schools like the University of Kentucky.

All of this was financed by Alice's unceasing efforts on her old Oliver #9 typewriter, sending letters around the country looking for donations to pay her students' way through school.

For all the years of work and dedication she gave, Alice asked only one thing in return from all her students: She would teach them for free if they would *promise to stay in the mountains with their education,* making their homes and communities a better place to live.

She made them promise to be *mountain leaders.*

Alice Lloyd passed away in 1962, nearly a half century after doctors told her she was dying. When she died, her personal estate was worth only sixteen cents.

Sixteen cents!

But her life was rich in accomplishments and blanketed in good work. She made a contribution to life around her of a magnitude rarely found in modern day America.

And she kept her promise to Abisha Johnson.

Alice Lloyd, my friends, is a Hero.

Miracle On Caney Creek

Words and Music by
Michael Johnathon

©1989 TechnoFolk Music Group/BMI
as performed on the CD "Troubadour"

Teeming in mountain history
Names that amaze and are so new to me
Traditions are old but the people are new
There's so much to learn on Caney Creek

The dreaming began when the vision was new
this gentle lady and her friend named June
gave hope to the people their children to teach
and started the Miracle on Caney Creek

People and mountains are free to be
Songs of the hills they keep singin' to me
If eagles can fly, Pippa could see
the Miracle on Caney Creek
the Miracle on Caney Creek

A two-room shack and some eggs to eat
a friend named 'Bysh and some wooden seats
old books on math and some on history
brought the young boys out to Caney Creek

The idea was simple and so easy to do
we'll trade education for the work that you do
promise a mountain leader you'll be
and you can stay on Caney Creek

People and mountains are free to be
songs of the hills they keep singin' to me
if eagles can fly, Pippa could see
the Miracle on Caney Creek
the Miracle on Caney Creek

In the studio while recording the chorus of Miracle On Caney Creek.

As with many stories, some facts become embellished with time. Most of Alice Lloyd's story is well documented and factual. One particular matter, however, was altered by Alice herself.

The accounts of Abisha Johnson, the money problems, the appearance on *This Is Your Life* are completely true. The depiction of her marriage is not. In reality, her husband, Arthur, moved to Kentucky with Alice and her mother in 1916. He was miserable there, and missed his life in Boston a great deal. He eventually began an illicit affair with a female volunteer who was recruited to help at the school. Alice soon found out about the relationship and confronted Arthur. This is when he tells her *"One life wasted is unavoidable, two lives wasted is senseless..."* The affair so humiliated Alice that she divorced Arthur immediately.

Strangely, he never did go back to Boston. Instead, he settled down with his new girlfriend just a few miles away near Prestonsburg, Kentucky. From then on, it was Alice's decision to completely wipe away Arthur's presence by claiming *he never came with her* to Kentucky to begin with. This is also the account she presented on national television during her NBC interview with Ralph Edwards.

Even so, this is a spectacular woman's story set in the most mysterious and romantic places in America. It is the spellbinding tale of a handicapped woman who overcomes insurmountable obstacles to help those around her.

During the writing of the *WoodSongs* book, Miracle On Caney Creek, Inc. was formed as an IRS approved, non-profit organization. The purpose of this group is to find the financing needed to turn Alice's story into a major motion picture.

Why do it this way and not work with a movie studio? Because I can't see taking Alice's story, her life of sacrifice and giving, and turning it over to a studio for profit. Alice's story belongs solely to the children of Appalachia.

The goal of Miracle On Caney Creek, Inc. is to produce the motion picture and assign *all* the proceeds to an Appalachian Students Tuition Fund, created in Alice Lloyd's memory. This fund will pay the tuition costs on behalf of poor Appalachian students, enabling them to attend the school of their choice.

You can be part of it by writing to:
Miracle On Caney Creek, PO Box 24187, Lexington, KY 40524

Appalachian Cornbread Salad
a recipe

This is *real* country cookin' that makes mealtimes for a quasi-semi-nearly-vegetarian like me a real corn-secrated experience.

This mountain dish came my way from some very good friends of mine. Jeanne Stewart, her daughter Jennifer and another good friend, Eileen Hassler, help organize the *Troubadour Concert Series*, held at the historic Paramount Arts Center in Ashland, Kentucky.

They've cooked for, hosted and fed everyone from Bill Monroe to Alison Krauss to Nanci Griffith to Waylon Jennings...and me. They stuffed this dish down my hungry throat one winter afternoon and I threatened my wife with drastic artist mood swings if she didn't add it to her culinary repertoire.

Now, I have yet another reason to look forward to coming home.

Mix one package of Hidden Valley Ranch dressing in a bowl with:

1 cup of milk
1 cup of sour cream
1 cup of mayonnaise

After you stir it up real good (with a spoon, not a mixer) set it in the 'fridge for 30 minutes. While the mix is chilling, bake yourself a normal pan of the best cornbread you can muster. Any recipe will do just fine. Then, get a package of frozen corn, boil it, then drain it. Get two cans of pinto beans, drain them.

Now, get a knife and slice the following:

3 fresh tomatoes	1/2 cup of fresh green bell peppers
1/2 cup of green onions	2 cups of shredded cheddar cheese

Grab your cornbread, crumble it up with your fingers and layer the bottom of a 9x13 inch pan with it. Next, layer the beans, peppers, and corn. Pour the dressing over the top. Add the tomatoes, onions and cheese. If you want to ruin this, you can also fry up a pound of bacon, let cool and then crumble on top. Stick this in the 'fridge for about an hour. Give me a plate of this and my sweet baby and there's absolutely no reason to ever leave home again.

Art, Songs & Poetry

As a songwriter and performer, I am often asked questions about how I write, where my songs come from, and what comes first, the music or the lyrics.

Good questions, but difficult to explain. Writing a song, poetry, even this book is a rather painful experience.

Writing *hurts.*

For those who don't write, this might sound a bit perplexing, so, bear with me. I'm going to try to describe and explain the writing process for you.

First, let me expound a bit on explanations I've heard from other artists. They range from the mundane, like Tom Petty's *"Oh, I kinda sit and just write 'em"* to the overtly spiritual and pretentious, *"The melodies come to me as cosmic gifts, floating through time and space and I capture them in my spirit,"* which I actually heard John Denver say to a concert audience in Louisville (I have often thought if Yanni died and came back as an acoustic guitar player, he'd be John Denver).

Anyway,

Those kinds of explanations sound really "artsy" and mysterious and help make the artist sound "special" and stuff, but certainly don't come close to answering the question.

The truth is, frankly, there is no mystery to writing. There are no cosmic spiritual influences helping the artist out. Art is a gift where talent is rarely, if ever, involved in creating it.

Why?

Because EVERYBODY creates art all the time. Every human being alive, even you, writes songs, creates poetry, paintings and books all the time. Saying an artist is "special" because he writes songs or might be a good painter is ridiculous. It's like saying they're special because they can breathe so good, or blink their eyes so well.

The natural course of human existence is to create, to transpose what we see in our mind into something physical, whether it be a sculpture, a painting, music or in words. And we all do this constantly.

My proof lies in the world of children.

Long before we became burdened with self-consciousness and stress, we ALL colored, we ALL made up our own songs, we ALL had fun sculpting with Play-doh and clay. We made up goofy stories and imaginary play friends. We even created games with rules we'd never heard of.

As children, art and the creation of it was a major part of our conscious and subconscious existence. Art is the essence of what makes us human.

Art is life.

Someone who says they *can't* write songs, paint, sing or write poetry is denying they are alive. Someone who believes they're special because they *can* needs to get their head out of that dark space between their knees.

Here is how I believe songs are written and how art is created, and it has everything to do with the human brain:

Our brains are separated into two distinctive sections. One part is a rather shallow, thin part of our conscious selves. Doctors say it makes up about 6-8% of our brain capacity. This is the part that allows us to be aware of what we are doing, thinking, planning, seeing, hearing, etc.

The other part, 94% of our brain, is a huge, dark cavernous arena of incredible depth and unknown power. Our subconscious self is the untappable, unexplainable portion of our brain that governs the myriads of functions our body accomplishes every second. It processes the overwhelming barrage of thoughts and memories and the organization of them. Our dreams and desires and senses are all born from here. You could harness the power of every computer ever made, hook them all up and still not even come close to the capacity or raw ability of one human brain. Our brain is so complex, in fact, that it defies our ability to understand it.

And, the brain is able to do one final function that a computer, no matter how powerful or advanced, can never do:

It can change its mind because it *feels* like it.

So, no matter how goofy, dumb, talentless or stupid you think you might be, you're in fact using one of the most powerful and amazing creations in the universe, a brain with unfathomable potential, to come to that ridiculous conclusion.

Your brain is an unquenchable creative well, constantly writing, singing, painting and giving birth to new ideas, whether you allow yourself to realize it or not.

And the key word here is *allow*.

Artists, very simply, are people who allow themselves to realize what their minds are creating, and then try to reproduce it into the physical world.

Understanding the process we use to create art is really quite simple. Since I'm a songwriter, let's use songwriting as our basic example, but keep in mind this principle holds true whether it's music, painting, poetry or book writing. The mind works the same, regardless.

Our brain is always writing songs.

It's always painting and writing poetry, too.

I'm talking about YOU, my friend. The songs, the art, that you create is stored forever in that huge, dark part of your subconscious mind.

As children, the gates between our two mental worlds opened wide and freely. It is the freedom that comes with the

Kids should be allowed to explore their imaginations with full freedom.

privilege of innocence. We "heard" the songs we wrote in our subconscious mind clearly and we sang them loudly, with no inhibitions. We closed our eyes and saw images and paintings and we pulled out our watercolors and crayons and had fun interpreting those visions to paper.

As kids, we had the *time* to keep them open.

As we grew older, the doors between those two worlds began to close. It happened as we became aware of what others thought of us. It happened as we became selfconscious about our image. It happened as we had less and less opportunities to open those doors.

We had *less time* to spend opening the gates.

We got involved in non-creative issues of life, and our minds eventually forgot how to get those gates opened again.

One of my favorite singers and songwriters ever, Harry Chapin, wrote a song about this very thing. It's called *Flowers are Red*. You can find the song on two albums, *Greatest Stories Live* and *Living Room Suite*. If you're a parent, I urge you to go out to a store, buy the CD and check out the words to this song. It's about a little kid whose gates were shut down tighter than a gnat's ass on an ice cube.

A quote from another philosopher comes to mind as well, and I think it's worth offering here:

> *"There is only one crime that cannot be forgiven, that of having poisoned the joys and destroyed the smile of a child..."*
> Maurice Maeterlinck

And yet another,

> *"In the end, we will preserve what we love, we will love what we understand, and we will understand what we are taught..."*
> Senegalese Wisdom

One of the greatest gifts a parent or teacher can give a child is freedom of expression. Sure, like everything in life, discipline and rules are best applied. But an adult who praises, encourages and helps a youngster keep those gates open will no doubt end up with a very happy, stable and well adjusted kid. Children whose gates are shut down early in life are usually miserable as adults.

Just because our gates have closed does not, however, mean our mind has stopped creating. To the contrary, it never stops. Some of these creations still surface in our dreams, or as confusing thoughts. But, unless our conscious mind can open those doors, the gates to our unconscious mind, we will never *hear* the songs we are writing, or *see* the painting we are creating.

Songwriters can go deep into their mind, literally think backwards, and bring songs forward through those gates into their conscious mind. An artist is someone who can open their own mental doors.

An artist is also someone who can bear the pain of creating.

Yes, writing a song hurts.

It's like muscles that lay dormant in your body, suddenly being used with force. I'm sure that, like anything else, the more the gates are opened, the less pain is involved. I also think that the more the gates are opened, the more aware you are of the pain, so it still hurts.

This is why so many songwriters and poets equate creating their art to giving birth. It hurts terribly until it's over, then you are totally in love with this new "child".

Let me quote some words by my friend Loretta Sawyer to help prove this point. It's from her poem *Thoughts On Writing*:

> ...*Writing can be torment*
> *Torment to find the right words to put on paper*
> *Writing can cause pain*
> *The pain of reality inside me*
> *But once completed it gives me great joy*
> *The joy of sharing myself with you...*

I once read an interview with songwriter James Taylor, who said he avoids writing because each song causes him so much pain as he's writing it.

And this analogy also proves my next point:

Just as children aren't born piece by piece, songs aren't created word by word or note by note.

They are delivered in completed form into the conscious world. It has been my conclusion, based on my own experience and those of my songwriting friends, that the mind will completely *pre-write* every note and word of a song before we ever hear it. You might *hear* the song in sections in the conscious mind, but it is passed along "whole" just the same.

Prolific songwriters, like Woody Guthrie or Bob Dylan, or authors like Steven King, have learned to prop those doors wide open all the time, and their brains send a torrent of creations forward to them. They can hear these songs and words clearly and have trained themselves to write it down as it happens.

Very often, we don't quite understand the meaning of what we create. This is a testament to the power of the inner mind. I remember when I wrote the song *Mountain*, the lyrics really confused me. I thought the song was about a homeless man, but it wasn't. The song took me less than ten minutes to write, literally gushing out of my head. I was quite surprised when it happened. But I couldn't understand the words and how they connected to each other, even though I was the one who wrote it. What does a hobo, a young girl and a middle aged woman have in common, I wondered?

I had to play the song to myself for a whole month before I realized I had written about different kinds of *emotional* homelessness, not just a homeless guy. A young girl abused by a parent might have a *house*, but it is not a *home*. A wife beaten by her husband might have a *house*, but again, it is not a *home*. They are just as homeless as a hobo in the park.

Well, now the song finally made sense.

A *ton* of sense.

The logic of the song wasn't a mistake, either. It was organized in the mind before I ever heard myself writing it. But I didn't *get it* until many weeks after the song was written.

I know literary writers and poets who go through the same thing. They write those words down, but don't quite understand them. Not right away. They actually have to learn from what they created *after* they write it.

Very often, the brain will unleash art forms from its dark

In concert on the stage of Alice Lloyd College

side that scares the pants off of us.

That's how powerful your mind is.

Just remember, the mind will always send the song forward in completed form. Like I said, you might only hear it piece by piece, buts it's there just the same. When a songwriter is sitting on his couch with guitar in hand, struggling through a songwriting episode, the best thing he can do is just completely relax and let the mind work. Many make the common mistake of viewing a song they are writing one word or note at a time. By doing this they are interfering with their ability to hear the song coming through their mental gates. They are allowing the conscious mind to intrude, to rewrite the song before they even get to hear it. Usually they just end up with lousy, unemotional songs.

Sometimes, stress or other stuff gets in the way of those gates opening. This is often called "writer's block". It's a very accurate term used when a songwriter or poet or painter goes through a period of time and *nothing* happens. They can't write. They think they've stopped creating. Their mental gates are blocked shut and they can't get them open.

Often, their reaction is to get scared.

The correct reaction is to relax instead. Let the mind rest a while. Those gates, so long as you are alive, will in fact reopen. And, when they do, you better be damned ready for it.

It's not uncommon for a writer to sit at a keyboard struggling, waiting, fretting over their lack of inspiration. Then those gates suddenly open up and words come gushing out of their head. It's like a mental volcanic eruption that goes from the mind through the hands to the fingers onto the keyboard and out on paper. Afterwards, they are left in a euphoric, literary orgasmic state of mind, happy but confused.

So, what happened?

The gates opened, that's all.

The inner mind had that story or poem or song completely pre-written, ready to go. Every word, paragraph and comma. They were lucky enough to be prepared when the doors opened and they caught it all at once.

Just like giving birth.

No mystery, no spiritual cosmic connection.

They just simply co-operate with their own head.

This section of the *WoodSongs* book is a good example. I knew I was gonna write this commentary for a while now. I waited for my head to feel ready, I sat down and I'm writing this straight through without stopping. My inner brain is telling my hands to write down every sentence and thought that it pre-wrote days or weeks ago. My gates are wide open and I'm having a blast doing this.

It works the same way with songwriting. Every note and chord change, even the poetry and melody is prewritten before we

162

get to hear it and write it down.

Can the *conscious* mind write a song?

Of course.

Commercial jingle writers do it all the time. But I wouldn't exactly call that art.

Country music is notorious for sticking writers into corporate writing cubicles from 9-5PM every day to write hit songs from basic formulas. Ever wonder why songs on country radio sound so...similar? It's because they're being written by "front-brained" writers in corporate situations. Some writers, like Steve Earle, Guy Clark, Lucinda Williams and Clint Black still write from the subconscious side, and their music is filled with unique imagery and musical changes. Their music doesn't sound formula at all.

Nashville is brimming with wonderful songwriters struggling within very sterile, corporate situations. They can't write what they feel, they have to write what sells. Many of them walk around Nashville with a musical front-brained lobotomy, unable to use the music that comes to them naturally. Country music is a magnificent art form, and I think it deserves better. It's time that the record companies take the lawyers and bean counters out of the music picture for a while, and let the musicians take their place at the creative controls. It will give country music a chance to breathe and grow again. It has stayed the same for too long, my friends. It has become corporate and sterile.

True art comes from deep inside our soul, from the very corridors of our intellect and our heart.

Songwriting is experienced that way.

When I write, I usually sit on a favorite rocking chair in my home and spend time just holding and strumming my Martin guitar for a while. I just relax and play anything...any sound, any chord structure. I love the warm, woody sound of the acoustic guitar so I just let the feeling and the tones wash over me like little ocean waves. Then you feel it happen. A chord on the guitar or a finger picking run jolts the mind awake, and the music starts coming forward. The inner mind actually starts *singing* to the conscious mind. Often, the lyrics come at the same time. Certain words imply a certain melody that fits the music patterns I'm playing on the guitar.

And a song is being written into the physical world.

It's real exciting.

And tiring.

And it hurts while it's happening, but I always feel great afterward. By listening from the inside out, so to speak, an artist is able to reveal what they feel by what they have created.

I also don't think it's an accident that many great songs are written in the morning, when the mind is rested and fully relaxed. Let me support this with a quote from my favorite writer, Henry David Thoreau:

All intelligence awakes with the morning.
Poetry and art, and the fairest and most memorable
actions of all men date from such an hour.
All poets and heroes emit their music at sunrise.
To him whose elastic and vigorous thought
keeps pace with the sun,
the day is perpetual morning..."

Thoreau is too cool...

The point here is simple: The more relaxed you are about entering your inner world, the faster those artistic gates will open. For many of us, our mind is most tranquil in the morning, before the day has a chance to fill it with mundane clutter.

And the results can be brilliant.

Here's a good example,

Around 1980, Bill Monroe was told he was dying of cancer. How sad this must have been for a man who was used to living life to its fullest. He created a new American art form and moved thousands of others to take up music as part of their lifestyle. He is rightfully called the *Father of Bluegrass,* and has used his life to make valuable contributions to the world of music and art.

As Mr. Monroe allowed the news of his illness to settle into his heart, his feelings were transposed by his mind. Early one morning, while sitting on an old chair on the front porch of his cabin home, he began playing a melody on his mandolin.

I don't know what power or force this man touched that day, maybe it was the sounds of the early mountain dawn, maybe it was his sadness, maybe it was the sight of the gray fog clinging to the sides of the mountain holler, but he wrote the most magnificent piece of music I've ever heard.

He expressed his feelings and fears about dying in a mandolin instrumental called *My Last Days On Earth.* This has got to be the most delicate and passionate music written in the twentieth century. You can find the song on the recent Bill Monroe compilation CD. It is majestic. Let me also add, that Bill ended up being OK. I've opened some shows with him a few times recently, he even signed my banjo. This past summer, he and Garth Brooks inducted Alison Krauss into the Grand Ole Opry *(I hear ol' Bill even goosed Alison backstage!).* As of this writing, he's 85 years young but not feeling too well.

OK, here's another and

Photo by Jon Sievert

The Father of Bluegrass, Bill Monroe.

more well known example,

Paul McCartney.

You know, the *cute* Beatle.

He woke up early one morning with this melody rolling around his head. Well, McCartney never heard this tune before nor did he have any words for it. But he liked it. Paul hummed it to John Lennon and several others, wondering if maybe he mistakenly assumed it was original, but actually ripped it off another songwriter. In fact, everyone he solicited opinions from confirmed that, Yes, Paul...you wrote it.

For several days, he would hum this tune and let it float in his mind. Frustrated, he used substitute lyrics inside the melody so he could sing the song.

"Scrambled eggs..." were the words he used.

More time passed, until his mind released the beautiful lyrics to *Yesterday,* and *Scrambled Eggs* was no more. That song has since become the most performed song in radio history...worldwide!

Can you follow what happened here?

Paul's mind wrote a song. He heard only the melody when he woke up one morning. He didn't freak or get upset. Instead, he relaxed and waited. Several days later, Paul, who trained himself as an artist to listen deep inside his mind, finally heard the lyrics and finished the song.

What does this mean?

It means he's rich and we're not.

It also means that art is a function of intelligent nature.

It means that *you* write songs.

Your *children* write songs.

Everybody writes songs.

Why could Beethoven, deaf as a granite rock, create musical masterpieces? Because music is written with the mind, not the ears. It is written deep in the subconscious mind, even while we are sleeping.

Why could Paul hear his song and you can't? Because you don't allow yourself the chance.

Period.

Who knows what magical masterpieces of art died hidden in the minds of timid souls? Think of the poetry, the paintings, the sculpture, the books and the music the world is missing because this majestic mental power was denied by its owner?

Songwriting is no more special than breathing, but it is a remarkable gift, a privilege, because not everyone exercises their ability.

In that way only, it is special.

So, when you see a young child singing freely in a hushed room, or scribbling furiously in a burst of colors on a bedroom wall, or telling you outlandish fibs and stories...be careful! Your reaction as a parent will determine whether those gates inside the child's mind stay open or be shut closed. No, I'm not implying you should let them write on a bedroom wall, either. I'm saying you should provide them with an abundance of good ways to express their artistic nature so they don't *need* the bedroom wall.

I have a little girl, Rachel.

I built her a special table we keep in the living room. This table is hers to color on. And I mean *on the table itself,* if she wants too. She spends hours on this table with clay, magic markers, watercolors and crayons. We hang her pictures all over the kitchen and give them to family as gifts. Sometimes she colors on paper, sometimes she colors past the paper onto the table, or sometimes she just colors on the table. As time goes by, that ol' table has absorbed quite a colorful personality. It's been a couple of years now, and you should see the explosion of colors on that thing!

It's beautiful!

Families across America should take a tip from folks in Appalachia. In older times, folks kept a guitar or banjo hanging on the wall. Anyone so moved could pull it down and share a song. What a happy sound for any house! Expression of art is not only fun, it also implies

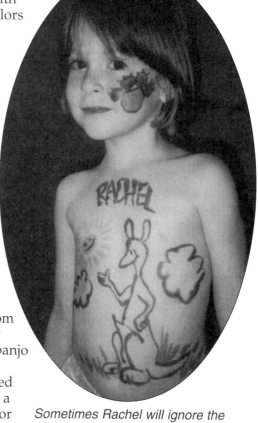

Sometimes Rachel will ignore the table and color on herself . . .

freedom. Freedom of spirit and of thought and of passion. What a great way of encouraging your kids to keep their gates wide open...

...and it beats the tail out of letting them watch MTV.

And, friends...I *hate* MTV.

音樂　　吉他　　玉絃琴

Northern Chinese words for music, guitar, and banjo.

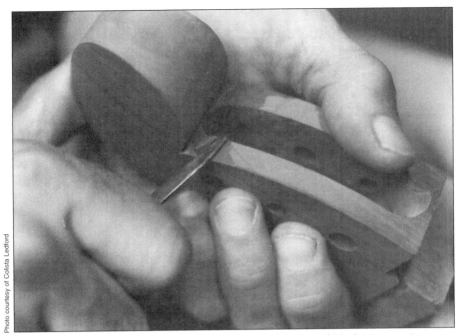

The hands of Homer Ledford as he crafts one of his instruments.

𝔚ood 𝔖ong

      I have a very good friend from Ireland, his name is Lochlain Feeley. He makes a good living as a high level corporate executive and gets to travel all over the world. He is also a passionate music lover, well versed in folksingers, songwriters and music history. He and I are constantly trading CDs and music magazines between the continents, and I always look forward to his visits to America so we can hang out.

      Lochlain is a good singer, a good guitar player and a free soul. He and I once had a very long transatlantic phone conversation about his frustrations at work, and how much he would just love to just quit, pack his guitar up in his car and motor through Europe.

      More than anything in the world, I wanted him to do just that.

      But, alas, people have responsibilities, bills and families to support. Lochlain made me realize how fortunate I am to be able to be a folksinger and make my living with my music.

      The song *WoodSong*, though not about Lochlain personally at all, was certainly inspired by the conversation we had that day.

      WoodSong is for everyone...

      ...every poet, sculptor, writer, dancer, musician, artist, painter and folksinger...who wanted to pursue their dreams and didn't.

WoodSong

Words and Music by
Michael Johnathon
©1995 Rachel-Aubrey Music/BMI, as performed on the CD "WoodSongs"

Photo by Warren Brunner

VERSE

You ain't the one ___ I re-mem-ber Some-thing hap-pened to you on the road, All your pas-sions have turned in-to ang-er Now it fol-lows wher-ev-er you go.

CHORUS

Life ain't for cow-ards and law-yers Dreams don't be-long to the rich Life is a song that's worth sing-ing

(inst.)

So pick up your songs and move on, Teach the whole world to hear a wood-song.

WoodSong

You ain't the one I remember
Something happened to you on the road
All your passions have turned into anger
Now it follows wherever you go

Why did you loose your direction
What made your heart sink so low
Where are the songs you were singing
And all of the poems you know?

Life ain't for cowards and lawyers
Dreams don't belong to the rich
Life is a song worth singing
So pick up your songs and move on
Teach the whole world to hear a WoodSong....

I see thunder beyond the horizon
And stars beyond all the clouds
Like water that falls from a mountain
And lands with a crash on the ground

Life ain't for cowards and critics
Try to do all they say can't be done
If you know a good song worth singing
Just pick up your voice and sing on
And teach the whole world to sing a WoodSong...

My 12 Favorite Albums

Here's a list of my twelve favorite albums. Sure, most of 'em are available on CD, but a couple aren't, so I use the word "album". Go figure. Anyway, I'm not listing them with a "Top Twelve" attitude nor am I trying to imply that number two is better than number five. I'm just listing them in random order as I think of them. Basically, if I was home on a Saturday night with a fire going and a glass of good merlot in my hand, this is the music I'd probably play.

Josh White at Town Hall
Josh White

Blue
Joni Mitchell

Harvest Moon
Neil Young

Precious Friends
Arlo Guthrie & Pete Seeger

Oh Mercy
Bob Dylan

Pete
Pete Seeger

Bringing It All Back Home: The Songs of Ireland
BBC-Various Artists- Double CD

Pet Sounds
Beach Boys

Dream Café
Greg Brown

Dublin Blues
Guy Clark

Homeless Brother
Don McLean

Arkansas Traveler
Michelle Shocked

My 12 Favorite Songs

Here is a list of my twelve favorite songs. In other words, these are the songs I would trade my soul for if only I could've written them. I'm not sure of my attraction to them; each seems completely different from the next to me. For whatever reason, I find them incredibly powerful. ESPECIALLY the Harry Chapin song. If you want to hear a two-minute song that will break your heart into a million pieces, then check it out.

My Last Days On Earth
Bill Monroe

(Sailing Down) My Golden River
Pete Seeger

New Wood
Si Kahn

Pastures of Plenty
Woody Guthrie

Blackwater
Jean Ritchie

Here Comes That Rainbow Again
Kris Kristofferson

Over the Mountain
Traditional

Vincent
Don McLean

Streets of London
Ralph McTell

Souveniers
Dan Fogelberg

The Shortest Story
Harry Chapin

Avé Maria
Bach

Songs & Albums I Learned the Most From

Here are the songs and albums that hit me over the head, shoved me off an emotional cliff, increased my musical ability, made me persevere, infused me with hope, changed my mind or showed me the way. They may not be my *favorite* songs or melodies, but they are important to my musical outlook just the same. Unless it's a song only, I've listed what I listen to the recording on *(vinyl Lp, CD or Cassette)* in case you want to find it.

I'm So Lonesome I Could Cry
Hank Williams

Circles and Seasons (Lp)
Pete Seeger

Aerial Boundaries (CD)
Michael Hedges

Lakes of Ponchartrain
Hothouse Flowers

Goin' Round This World (Lp)
Dave Evans

Together Again (Lp)
The Weavers

Hymn
Janis Ian with Odetta

Tomorrow Lies in a Cradle
Fred Hellerman

Blind Willie McTell
Bob Dylan

Graceland (CD)
Paul Simon

Across the Universe
John Lennon

Live at the Royal Albert Hall (Cassette)
Ralph McTell

General Store

WoodSongs is a celebration of American music old and new. Fourteen acoustic songs, including the spoken poem *Weaver and the Wood*, go from traditional folk (Uncle Dave Macon's *Over the Mountain*) to progressive bluegrass (*Shady Grove, Mr. Bojangles*) to originals (*Colista's Jam, Summer Honeymoon, Mousie HiWay*). Album standouts include *Summer Honeymoon*, an original song destined to be a classic, with it's trombone trio, the album title song *WoodSong*, a gutsy banjo rendition of Woody Guthrie's *Pastures of Plenty*, the energy of the live version of *Mousie HiWay*, Michael's tribute to his Appalachian home and the plaintive Irish classic *Mountains O' Mourne*. Guest artists include:

Appalachian dulcimer legend	Grammy winning banjo master	Traditional mountain musician
Jean Ritchie	**J.D. Crowe**	**Homer Ledford**

The 1995 release by Michael Johnathon includes twelve acoustic songs and a spoken poem. The album highlight is the beautiful duet with the legendary ODETTA on the song *New Wood (gone, gonna rise again)*. Original songs include *Already Gone, Flyin', The Room, Windows, Pirate, The Accusation* and the title track. Banjo songs include Bob Dylan's *Masters of War*, and Michael's two originals *Mousie HiWay* and *Cosmic Banjo* (recorded with a French horn quartet). Includes song keys and tunings.

The very controversial album hailed by music critics as a "...masterpiece". Michael recorded this album with the best acoustic players in Nashville and L.A., plus a full 61-piece symphony! Eleven songs include *Seasons, Freedom, Mark of the Maker, Young & Alone*. Highlights include the beautiful ballad *Walden: The Ballad of Thoreau, The Dream* (recorded with four choirs in four different languages), *Techno-Folk* (Michael, his banjo, a rock band...and a symphony) and *Secrets in the Key of G* (recorded LIVE with a string quartet).

Order the complete "Folk Trilogy" on CD or cassette, your choice!

WoodSongs, Assassins in the Kingdom and *Dreams of Fire*
for just $24.50 plus $3.50 shipping and we will send you
Troubadour for FREE! You will get ALL FOUR albums for this one price!

Michael's first album. This CD spawned three music videos which aired on TNN and CMT. This is Michael's "album of voices." Songs include the musical earth poem *Water of Life* (recorded with 800 teenagers in Charleston, WV), *WagonStar* (recorded with 1,000 young people in Frankfort, KY), and the moving Appalachian song *Miracle On Caney Creek* (with over 200 children). Other songs include *Indian Dream, The Passing, Troubadour,* and more.

Miracle on Caney Creek, the story of Alice Lloyd as described in this book. Thirty minute VHS docu-drama includes the *Miracle On Caney Creek* music video.

The magnificent Odetta sings the duet *New Wood* with Michael on the album *Assassins in the Kingdom*

ORDERING INFORMATION

FOLK TRILOGY: Order the complete folk trilogy (*WoodSongs, Assassins in the Kingdom* and *Dreams of Fire*) and we will include the *Troubadour* album **FREE!** You will receive all four albums for just $24.50 (plus $3.50 shipping), CD or cassette, your choice.

SINGLE ALBUM ORDERS: To receive any *single* album, enclose a check or money order of $15 for <u>each</u> CD or $11 for <u>each</u> Cassette (plus $1.50 shipping).

WOODSONGS BOOK: Additional copies of this book are $16.95 each, or $14.50 each with a music and/or video order (plus $2.50 shipping).

MIRACLE ON CANEY CREEK VIDEO: Just $14.50 each (plus $2.50 shipping).

SHIPPING INFORMATION: Order any three items (ie: "Folk Trilogy" + WoodSongs book + video) and your total shipping will only be $4.00 in the continental USA.

Make check or money order payable to
PoetMan Records, USA, P.O. Box 24187, Lexington, KY 40524-4187

Acknowledgements & "I Know I Owe You"s!

One person alone can't accomplish a thing in this world.
That's no less true when writing a book.
My biggest "thank you" goes to Jenny...my friend, my editor, partner, receptionist, public relation's representative and gatekeeper to my soul.

Also, to **Oscar and Scott Rucker** at North American Imprints for making this book possible. And to my friend **Susan Hamilton** for introducing me to Oscar and guiding the project along with us.
To **Toshi Seeger, Tammy Farley and Tabitha Carnes** for catching all kinds of goofy mistakes in the post-edit, pre-publication reads that makes me look like I are a better writer, even though we all know I isn't...
To **Tammy Farley** for being the world's best cheering section, Board member and numbers cruncher, and to **Mark** for putting up with it.
To **Jeanne & Jennifer Stewart, Eileen Hassler, Rick Rushing, Corday Lee, Rob McNurlin** and all my friends in the Troubadour Family.
To **Tamara Hackney, Jim Jones** and crew at Graphic Film in Lexington. Thanks for putting up with my bad jokes and getting this done for me.
To my friend **Art Fegan** and everyone at Gurtman & Murtha for giving me those stages to play on.

And to those who I just can't do without:
Joe Garnett, Carolyn Embry, Homer and Colista Ledford, Don McLean, Jean Ritchie and George Pickow, my friend Odetta, Pete and Toshi Seeger, Lochlain Feeley, Loretta Sawyer, my Bud buddies (**Tony Gaughan, Guy Spriggs** and **Jim Bohannon III**), James Crisp, John Roberts, Lucy Locke and the library staff of **Alice Lloyd College, David and Jo Rita Gates, Ron Daley, Rick Marks,** everyone at **PoetMan Records USA** and **Pinecastle Records, Tom Martin** and my friends at WVLK and all the radio folks around the country who play my records.
And finally,
To **Melody Larkin** and **Rachel Aubrey**...I do love you so.

Information Sources:

WoodSongs Folk Newsletter & General Store
IT'S FREE! Send a SASE to:
PO Box 24187, Lexington, KY 40524

Odetta
c/o Leonard Rosenfeld Mngt.
15 W 84th St., New York, NY 10024

Jean Ritchie new CD, Mountain Born
c/o Greenhays Recordings
7A Locust Ave., Port Washington, NY 10050

Homer Ledford
dulcimer and instrument maker
125 Sunset Heights, Winchester, KY 40391

Acoustic Musician Magazine
PO Box 1349, New Market, VA 22844

Sing Out! Folk Magazine
PO Box 5253, Bethlehem, PA 18015-0253

5-String Quarterly Banjo Magazine
8407 Loralinda Drive, Austin, TX 78753

The Clearwater Environmental Organization
112 Market Street, Poughkeepsie, NY 12601

Troublesome Creek Times
"The world's best weekly newspaper in Appalachia, Under One Million Sold!"
PO Box 700, Hindman, KY 41822 (subscriptions: $17 per year, post paid)

Edited by Rachel's mom with lots of help from Toshi Seeger.

176